# SAVING OUR SONS

# S.O.S
## Saving Our Sons

*Confronting the Lure of Islam*

*with Truth, Faith & Courage*

CARL ELLIS, EDITOR

———

with DON DAVIS, PASTOR R. C. SMITH

and an AFTERWORD BY WILFORD DARDEN

IMANI (i) BOOKS

CHICAGO, ILLINOIS

Publisher
Imani Books
342 Broadway, Suite 428
NY, NY 10013
1-800-860-8642
www.imanibooks.net <http://www.imanibooks.net/>

First Edition
First Printing

LIBRARY OF CONGRESS CATALOGING-IN-PUBLICATION DATA

*Saving Our Sons*/Carl Ellis, Jr.
Includes bibliographical references
ISBN-13: 978-1-934056-74-5
ISBN-10: 1-934056-74-X
1. Religion 2. Islam

Library of Congress Control Number: 2007940977

Printed in the United States of America.

*Thanks to Lela Gilbert for her conceptual and editorial contributions to this book*

# CONTENTS

# INTRODUCTION

W E LIVE IN a pivotal time in history. Never before has the opportunity for Christians to carry out the "Great Commission" been so great. Yet, never before has the Church faced such great challenges. The proliferation of competing worldviews today is staggering. One of the greatest issues we face in the Church is the explosive growth of Islam in our communities. If we take the rise of Islam seriously, it will be an opportunity for ministry. If we continue to ignore this Islamic challenge, it will prove to be more than a challenge—Islam will eventually overtake our community.

The events of September 11, 2001, were a rude awakening for all of us. Sadly, it appears that we have resumed our cultural slumber. Today, we face a cacophony of conflicting voices claiming to articulate the true nature of Islam. Is it a religion of peace or a faith of violence and war? Is it compatible with Christianity or anti-Christian? It is crucial to understand the truth about Islam because it is making a global effort to convert our communities and our world to its belief system.

Our Lord commands us to be salt and light in the world. Yet, often our Muslim friends are more faithful to their global mission than we are to ours. Their prime directive is to get the world to embrace Islam by any means necessary while we in the Christian Church are frequently preoccupied with private salvation, almost to the exclusion of concern for our community's legitimate social issues. We can't blame Islam for taking advantage of a vacuum we've created. How are we addressing issues of concern to our emerging generations—issues such as identity, pain, rage and the quest for true manhood? The Bible is twice as rich as the Qur'an concerning righteousness, social justice and compassion for the poor. Yet the Muslims have gained a reputation of being twice as rich as we are in implementing these principles.

Sure, the Christian Church continues to be the strongest institution in the African-American community. But will it remain so? One hundred years ago, the Christian Church comprised the *majority* of Americans. Today, it involves many, but not most of us. Who is filling the gap? The Muslim community is definitely striving to increase its influence. How else can we explain why so many African-American young men are attracted to Islam—young men who were often raised in our Church? In fact, most American converts to Islam identify themselves as former Christians. How can we correct this trend?

It is not enough to lament the current state of affairs. Ignoring Islam's infiltration is no solution. Neither is taking cheap shots at the Islamic community. We need to objectively look at our community's needs—specifically our young men's needs—and develop a fresh scriptural approach to addressing them. We must outfit our youth with the necessary tools to resist the pull of Islam. We also need to equip ourselves with training and skills to successfully minister to those in the grip of Islam. It is my prayer that this manual will help accomplish these goals.

Whatever we may say about the Islamic influence we face in our community, one thing is certain: without it, we may not have awakened to the necessity of rediscovering our rich biblical and theological heritage. It has given us an opportunity to reexamine our faith and practice.

# 1

## FACING THE FACTS

*Los Angeles Sentinel,* JUNE 17-23, 2004

LOS ANGELES—After Vicky Lindsay lost her oldest son Lionel in a South-Central Los Angeles shooting incident, she was determined to protect his little brother, her only surviving child. In an interview with the L.A. Sentinel, the African-American single mom said, "As a mother who has lost her child and not wanting to lose another one, we are desperately searching for anybody, anywhere, anyway who can help us keep our babies alive and being that our churches will not step out and Minister Tony is the only one who gets out of his seat and into the streets, we felt the need to go to him."

Minister Tony Muhammad, the western regional minister for the Nation of Islam, responded to Ms. Lindsay's and other mothers' appeals. He "immediately put a call out through radio—one week before Mother's Day—for mothers to bring their sons, ages 5 to 18 to Muhammad Mosque for manhood training."

Of the Peacemakers Junior Fruit Manhood Training program, which he organized at the mosque, Min. Muhammad said, "There's nothing worse than a mother's cry, her wish to save her son and keep him out of harm's way. I can only reflect on the Minister (Farrakhan) saying 'make all men and boys join the Fruit of Islam.'"

In June 2004, over 150 mothers had responded.

*Los Angeles Wave,* MARCH 17, 2005

INGLEWOOD—A group that includes Minister Tony Muhammad from the Nation of Islam has begun the application process to establish a charter school in Inglewood. A public hearing on the matter was discussed during the March 9 meeting of the Inglewood school board.

The founders of the Nation's DIGNITY (Developing the Individual Greatness Needed in Today's Youth) Charter School are husband and wife Trina and Walter Muhammad, and Minister Tony Muhammad, western regional minister of the Nation of Islam based in Los Angeles. . .

No members of the school board nor Superintendent Pamela Short-Powell could be reached for comment.

"I am a Muslim woman, but the Nation of Islam is not applying for the charter," Trina Muhammad said. The public "may think it's a Muslim school or a religious entity, but it's not. It's a charter school. . .

"[Tony Muhammad] wants to focus on the young men and keep them out of gangs, be a mentor to them," Trina Muhammad said.

During its first year the charter school will serve a minimum of 340 students in kindergarten through the fifth grade. Each year the school will expand one grade until the school serves eight graders as well.

*Los Angeles Wave*, APRIL 28, 2005

SOUTH LOS ANGELES—During a forum this week on racially motivated violence at Jefferson High School, the president of the school's Black Student Union said that she, like a number of other African-American students, was considering leaving the school for good out of fear of being "jumped."

Meanwhile, Minister Tony Muhammad of the Nation of Islam pledged protection to students who feel threatened by what is described as a growing, palpable tension between Blacks and Latinos on the campus.

THESE THREE NEWS stories make one disturbing point: determined and tenacious members of Nation of Islam, such as Minister Tony Muhammad in Los Angeles, are hard at work in our African-American communities. Throughout the United States both the Nation of Islam and orthodox Muslim mosques have targeted our youth—and specifically our sons—for conversion to their religion and their causes. We need to recognize this reality. And we need to do all we can to save our sons from its grasp.

It is important, as we begin, for us to understand that although followers of Nation of Islam and more traditional Islamic groups both identify themselves as Muslims, they are not one and the same. Groups like Nation of Islam accept beliefs that are heretical to orthodox Islam. They worship at different mosques and follow different traditions. But as we will see, many African Americans who started their journey into Muslim beliefs and practices by following Nation of Islam and its leaders have found their way into more traditional forms of Islam. And too often they end up in radicalized groups with violent goals.

In America's urban communities—including our churches—there are three typical responses to Islam:

1. Denial
2. Coexistence
3. Fear

The time has come for our churches to understand Islam and, in the right spirit, to take appropriate action. Whether you are a pastor, a parent or a prayer partner, we hope to equip you to meet Islam's challenge with a fourth, different response: faith, truth and courage.

If we are to save our communities, we need to begin by *saving our sons*. We need not only save them from the dangers of the world, the seductions of the flesh and the temptations of the Devil. We need to respond to Islam's efforts to rob us of our sons—efforts that seek to take them away from our community and from the true knowledge of God through His Son Jesus Christ.

*Consider these facts:*

❖ Whether in their neighborhoods or in prisons, African-American men are 150 percent more likely to convert to Islam than other Americans.
❖ Seven out of ten conversions in U.S. prisons are to Islam. Although official Islamic prison chaplains are orthodox Muslims, there are several unofficial forms of Nation of Islam being proselytized to inmates.
❖ 1.5 to 2 million African Americans are Muslim, 90 percent of whom consider themselves former Christians.
❖ 60 percent – 70 percent of American traditional Muslims came out of Nation of Islam, many into far more radicalized forms of Islam.

As African-American Christians, we need to find clear answers to five key questions:

*What is Islam?*
*How can we protect our churches from Islam's challenge?*
*How did Islam develop in the African-American community?*
*How should the Christian community respond to Islam?*
*What should be the Christian community's long-term goals?*

In the chapters that follow, we will look closely at these questions. We hope you'll ask the Lord for his wisdom and strength as you prayerfully consider some of the facts, suggestions and ideas presented here. We pray that you will identify specific ways you can begin to address Islam's ever-growing challenge to our congregations and communities.

## *Chapter One Discussion Questions:*

1. Of the three typical responses to Islam in Christian communities, which one do you think is the most common: denial, coexistence or fear? Why? Can you think of an example?
2. Of these three responses, which do you believe to be the most dangerous to the Christian community? Discuss why it is a threat.
3. What worries you most about Islam's outreach into Christian communities?
4. Why do you think young African-American prisoners are particularly open to Muslim proselytizing?
5. Do you believe that the Christian community has failed young African-American men? Why or why not?
6. Which poses the greatest threat to your community: Nation of Islam's (various forms of) outreach programs or efforts made by orthodox Islamic mosques?

# 2

## WHAT IS ISLAM?

ISLAM IS ONE of the fastest growing religions in the world. Some estimate its annual growth to be about 2.75 percent. Most of this growth is biological: the birth rate among Muslims is higher than among non-Muslims, especially in the West. One out of every five people in the world today is Muslim—about 1.2 billion. Today, there is a comprehensive plan to Islamicize the United States and the West. In fact, according to the United Kingdom's Barnabus Fund, since 1973 the Organization of the Islamic Conference has spent over $100 billion in this effort.

### DA'WA—ISLAMIC MISSIONS

MUSLIMS HAVE ALWAYS believed it to be their duty to spread the knowledge of Allah. They call this *da'wa*. They consider Islam superior to all other religions, and Muslims believe themselves to be a blessing of mercy to the world. They often site the following Qur'anic verse:

*We sent thee not, but*
*As a blessing for all creatures.*
*(Surah 21:107)*

Devout Muslims feel it is their duty to persuade non-Muslims to submit to Allah and His Messenger by any means necessary, including discussion, preaching, economic incentives and—in some circumstances—the sword.

## THE GROWING ISLAMIC PRESENCE IN THE UNITED STATES

GWENDOLYN X (Gwendolyn J. Carter) writes:

I grew up in an Islamic home in Philadelphia, Pennsylvania. My parents and our community of Muslims gave me a great feeling of security as a young child. The Muslim brothers and sisters engulfed my family with encouragement, moral support and praise. They also played important leadership roles in our neighborhood.

We attended the mosque faithfully and were frisked each time we entered. I remember being indoctrinated with words like, "I believe in one God whose proper name is Allah"; "I believe in the Holy Qur'an and in the Scriptures of all the prophets of God"; and "I believe in the truth of the Bible, but I believe it has been tampered with and must be reinterpreted so that mankind will not be snared by the falsehoods added to it." I remember joining with other children my age singing, marching and chanting "M-U-H-A-M-M-A-D." I remember hearing over and over, "The White man is the devil—we should never trust him." I also remember comic strips depicting the White man with a forked tongue, a tail, horns on his head and a false smile.

My father left the Nation of Islam for reasons never communicated to me. I believe he was reprimanded for smoking and left because of the strict discipline. Not long after this, my parents' marriage fell apart. My mother left my dad, taking her three Muslim children with her. Later, our family reunited. It lasted almost two years. During this time my baby brother was born. The next time my parents separated, we moved south to live with my mother's parents. This turned out to be a means God used to expose me to the truth of Jesus Christ.

We lived in a small Alabama town, about seventy-five miles from the nearest mosque. I attended my grandmother's AME Church for eight years. Yet I never understood what I heard. I watched preachers "whoop," and sisters shout and fall down. My mother told me to sit and not listen to what was said. This sparked a real curiosity in me to know what was being said.

While in the twelfth grade, I visited my sister at Tuskegee University. I attended a "Jesus Rally" sponsored by the Navigators, a Christian para-church ministry. For the first time I understood the Gospel. The Black brothers had tears screaming down their faces as they talked of how God had transformed them. I believed I was a "good" person. I was a Muslim. I went to church. I even gave money and sang in the choir. Hearing "all my righteousness was as filthy rags with maggots crawling over it" crushed me. Yet somehow I knew this was true. For the first time I saw my real need for this Jesus who loved me and died for me. I asked God to forgive me for trying to run my own life and surrendered myself to Him.

The hatred I learned had bogged down my desire to advance my people. Now that I am free from hatred, this desire is gratified. The Bible includes all races when it says, "For God so loved the world that He gave His only Son" (John 3:16a).

I know now that even as a child, born into the Nation of Islam, God was already bringing me to Himself. Many of the disciplines learned as a Muslim continue to enhance my life in Christ.

The formative years of a child's life are important. As a child,

I only knew programming. Today as an educator and mother, I practice Solomon's wise saying, "Train a child in the way he should go, and when he is old he will not turn from it" (Proverbs 22:6). My husband and I are committed to train our children in the righteousness of Christ, not to program them. "As for me and my household, we will serve the Lord" (Joshua 24:15).

ACCORDING TO A 2007 Pew Research Center survey, the total Muslim-American population is estimated at 2.35 million, "based on data from this survey and available Census Bureau data on immigrants' nativity and nationality. It is important to note that both of these estimates are approximations." Islam claims to be America's fastest growing religion, although exact numbers to support this statement do not exist. As for what proportion of American Muslims are African American, the same Pew survey states that "estimates of the proportion of native-born Muslims who are African American range from 20% to 42%."

San Francisco State University reports, "African Americans are one of the fastest-growing segments of the Muslim population in the U.S. Given the dearth of demographic data on American Muslims in general, estimates of the number of African American Muslims vary widely. . . . A 2001 survey of 416 mosques in the U.S., coordinated by Hartford Seminary's Hartford Institute for Religious Research, found that about 30% of mosque-goers were African American."

Most African-American converts to Islam describe themselves as former Christians. In many cases, they were dissatisfied with their church experience and searching for an authentic religious faith. They saw in Islam an apparent fulfillment of their search. However, because their knowledge of Islam was limited, they imported many of their Christian instincts into their Muslim faith. When these converts to Islam are asked why they left Christianity, their answers are remarkably consistent: "Christianity did not answer my questions or address my issues."

Ironically, these questions and issues are thoroughly answered and addressed in the Bible. The problem is that we in the American Church have too often neglected the scripture that addresses their concerns. Of 1 to 1.5 million African-American Muslims, only about twenty thousand are members of Louis Farrakhan's Nation of Islam. In fact, if we group all the Black Nationalist–oriented Muslims together, their total would be a maximum of two hundred thousand. Thus, the overwhelming majority of African-American Muslims are orthodox, or mainline.

## MUHAMMAD, THE FOUNDER OF THE ISLAMIC FAITH

LET'S TAKE TIME to learn some basic facts about orthodox Islam.

According to Islamic tradition, Muhammad was born in A.D. 570 in Mecca, an international trade center in what is now Saudi Arabia. His father died just before Muhammad's birth; his mother died when he was about five. The boy was raised by relatives and became a camel driver.

In the year 610, at the age of forty, Muhammad was meditating in a mountain cave when he had what he claimed was the first of many revelations from God, carried to him by the archangel Gabriel. These revelations are understood to have been the direct utterances of Allah—the direct speech of God. For the next twenty-three years, Muhammad received these revelations and preached them publicly. Since Muhammad was illiterate, he recited the words to scribes who wrote them down. These words were recorded and collected in what we now call the Qur'an.

Muhammad died in 632 and was buried in Medina. After his death, conflicts over who should be his successor led to factions within Islam, including Sunnis and Shi'as (also called Shiites), which together make up about 95 percent of the world's Muslims.

## SUNNIS VS. SHI'ITES

AFTER THE DEATH of Muhammad, his closest companions chose Abu Bakr as the first caliph after Muhammad. Abu Bakr was the father of Aisha, Muhammad's second wife. Aisha was about six or seven years old when Muhammad married her and about seven or eight when he consummated the marriage. Most Muslims accepted the selection of Abu Bakr.

A small group of Muslims supported the traditional tribal idea of a bloodline succession to Muhammad. Therefore, they opposed the selection of Abu Bakr and rallied around Ali, Muhammad's cousin and son-in-law. Muhammad had no sons; Ali was married to Fatima, Muhammad's daughter, so Ali was his closest male heir.

Those who supported Abu Bakr and rejected Ali and his divine right to the caliphate were called Sunnis (meaning "the way of the prophet"). They advocated the concept of leadership by the caliph. The caliphate concept is an executive type of leadership. Eventually, the Sunni caliphate was divided into four schools of jurisprudence: *Hanafi, Hanbali, Maliki* and *Shafi.*

Those who supported Ali were called Shi'ites (meaning "party of Ali"). They advocated the concept of leadership by the imam. The imamate concept reflects a belief that humanity is always in need of a divinely ordained leader and authoritative teacher in all religious matters—a teacher who is fully immune from sin and error.

## THE *QUR'AN*

ACCORDING TO ISLAMIC tradition, the source of the Qur'an is the Eternal Tablet. This tablet sits at the right-hand side of Allah's throne. It has 114 divisions that have been sent down throughout human history. One hundred of these divisions no longer survive. Ten were sent down to Adam, fifty were sent down to Seth, thirty were sent down to Enoch and ten were sent down to Abraham. As we've seen, the four surviving divisions are:

1. The Law, or Torah, sent down to Moses
2. The Psalms, or Zabur, sent down to David
3. The Gospel, or Injil, sent down to Jesus
4. The Qur'an, sent down to Muhammad

## MUSLIM BELIEFS—*IMAN*

### Belief in God (Allah)

Allah is one, having no partners and no equals. According to many orthodox theologians, Allah's otherness keeps humankind from knowing Him. Many Muslims assert that they, the Christians and the Jews worship the same God. It is true that "Allah" is the Arabic word for God and Arabic-speaking Christians refer to God as Allah.

### Belief in Angels and Demons (Mala'ik *And* Jinn)

According to Islamic teaching, Allah created angels from light, man from clots of blood and demons from fire. Some demons became Muslims when they heard the recitations. These jinns are believed to be beneficent, while the non-Muslim jinns can cause much harm.

### Belief in the Holy Books (Kutub)

Islam's holy books include the Torah (the Law), the Psalms, the Gospels, and the Qur'an. All these revelations are believed to have been corrupted except for the Qur'an, which is seen as the final revelation—the completion and correction of all previous revelations.

## Belief in the "Prophets Of God" (Rusal)

Muslims believe that there have been 124,000 prophets in the history of mankind. Muhammad is considered the last and the greatest of them. Jesus is also included, but only as one of many prophets.

## Belief in the "Decrees Of God" (Yaum Ul'akhir)

Because Allah is sovereign, Muslims believe He is responsible for everything that happens. He decides the fate of men and angels, and is responsible for good and evil. Muslims often call this "predestination"; however, we believe "fatalism" is a more accurate term for their concept of predestination.

## Belief in the "Day of Judgment" (Qiyamah)

Muslims believe that salvation is available through the belief that Allah is one and Muhammad is his prophet. Muslim practices (called the Five Pillars of Islam) are voluntary expressions of this belief. Those who have not acknowledged these beliefs and practices will be condemned to suffer in hell as infidels by Allah on the Day of Judgment.

Christians, by contrast, believe in redemption. The "wages" of sin are death—both physical and eternal—but through Christ's death on the cross and His resurrection, the wages of sin have been paid, and death has been defeated. By placing their faith in Jesus's redemptive work, Christians receive bodily resurrection from the dead and eternal life, which amounts to salvation at the Last Judgment: "There is now no condemnation for those who are in Christ Jesus, because through Christ Jesus the law of the Spirit of life set me free from the law of sin and death" (Romans 8:1).

# HOW THE QUR'AN WAS COMPILED

THE ARABIC WORD *qur'an* means "recite." Muhammad died in A.D. 632. His followers had memorized parts of what he had said and these were written down, although different followers recited different versions of his recitations. Muhammad himself claimed that Allah had given him seven different versions of each recitation.

The Battle of Aqaba (A.D. 633) resulted in the death of most of the best reciters. This created a crisis for the Muslim community. They were about to lose the words of their prophet.

Abu Bakr became the first caliph after the death of Muhammad. He ruled from 632 to 634 A.D. After the Battle of Yamama in 632, he gathered the written versions of Muhammad's recitations and had scribes record what the remaining reciters remembered. There continued to be disputes and eventually Muslims were killing Muslims over the different versions of Muhammad's recitations, which we now know as the Qur'an.

Uthman ibn Afan became the third caliph after Muhammad. He ruled from A.D. 644 to 656. Uthman collected all remaining Qur'anic manuscripts, and had a committee edit them. He then burned all variant versions of the Qur'an. The result was the "Uthmanic Version," the Qur'an that is in use today.

# THE ORGANIZATION OF THE QUR'AN

THE QUR'AN HAS 114 surahs (chapters). They are arranged according to importance and length, from longest to shortest, the first surah being the only exception. Each surah has a title from an event in it. The first eighty-six surahs tend to be lofty, spiritual, pure, tolerant and concerned with social justice. The twenty-eight later surahs, recited in Mecca, tend to be pragmatic, community oriented, harsh and militaristic—endorsing war and repressive measures toward non-Muslims to advance Islam.

# THE HADITH
## (TRADITIONS OF THE PROPHET)

AFTER THE DEATH of Muhammad, the best authorities on what Muhammad did and said were his *sahabis* (companions). The accounts of Muhammad and his companions are compiled in a collection called the Hadith. The Hadith is considered a supplement to and clarification of the Qur'an.

Structurally, the Hadith has two parts:

1. *Isnad* (the "support"), "the chain of witnesses"
2. *Matn* (the "substance"), the actual information

The Hadith covers subjects including *halal* (what is allowed), *haram* (what is forbidden), religious obligations and various Islamic laws. It addresses doctrines about hell, paradise, angels, creation and revelation.

# SORTING OUT THE HADITH

As ISLAM SPREAD to various cultures, words and deeds ascribed to Muhammad became voluminous. In response, Muslim scholars established rules by which false Hadith would be separated from true Hadith. They classified the Hadith in relation to Muhammad as follows:

1. *Sahih* (meaning "sound")—These fulfilled all the requirements of a true Hadith.
2. *Hassan* (meaning "fair")—Some of the "witnesses" were

either not known or had no direct relationship with Muhammad or his companions.

3. *Da'if* (meaning "weak")—These were judged to have suspicious content or unreliable authority.

Sunni Muslims have six Hadith collections. The *Al Bukhari Hadith* is considered by Sunnis to be the most reliable.

Shi'ite Muslims have five Hadith collections called the *Akhbar*. Shi'ites do not accept any of the six Hadith collections of the Sunni Muslims.

# MUSLIM PRACTICES—*DIN*

THE PRACTICES OF Islam are very important to Muslims, and in the Qur'anic references to the scales of judgment, Heaven is achieved if one's good deeds outweigh one's bad deeds. This explains the Muslim necessity for doing things precisely according to Islamic law, as a means of gaining merit. Muslim practices cover many aspects of life. The basic ones are called the Five Pillars of Islam. They are as follows:

1. *Shahada* (the creed)
   It states, "There is no God but God and Muhammad is the messenger of God."

2. *Salat* (prayers)
   Five times of prayer a day is the established practice in Islam. These times are 1) morning, 2) noon-time, 3) mid-afternoon, 4) sunset and 5) between sunset and retiring for sleep.

3. *Zakat* (alms-giving)
   A Muslim is encouraged to give $2\frac{1}{2}$ percent of his gross worth for the poor and for the propagation of Islam.

4. *Sawm* (fasting)

During the lunar month of Ramadan, no food or drink is to pass a Muslim's lips from sunrise to sunset. Ramadan is also characterized by great socializing and feasting during the evening hours.

5. *Hajj* (pilgrimage to Mecca)

Islam teaches that the pilgrimage to Mecca must be made once in a lifetime if possible.

### *Jihad (holy war)*

Although it is not officially among the Five Pillars of Islam, jihad is a universal belief among Muslims and some do consider it to be the sixth pillar.

There are several interpretations of the jihad concept but, to put it in simple terms, most scholars maintain that:

❖ *Inner jihad* is fought spiritually, against sin in oneself.
❖ *Outer jihad* is fought physically, against the external enemies of Islam, namely, non-Muslims. (We also see around us another innovation of radical Islam: jihad against other Muslims.)

We continually see evidence of this second type of Islam in the news, as self-declared armies of Allah perform terrorist acts in order to establish a Pan-Islamic Empire. Usama bin Laden has called for "jihad against the *kuffar* [unbelievers] in every part of the world."

# TWO MAJOR CHARACTERISTICS OF ISLAM

### A. *Ummah*

Ummah means the worldwide community of Muslims. All Muslims are presumed to belong to the Ummah, which gives them a binding sense of community. The Ummah is their basis of group identity and validation and provides accountability for observance of the Five Pillars.

This is different from the spiritual Body of Christ to which Christians belong, based on a personal faith in Jesus Christ and unity in His Spirit. It is not related to external religious affiliation.

B. *Sunnah*

Sunnah describes the Muslim community's proper way of life, based on the sayings and doings of Muhammad. The rules for this lifestyle are primarily derived from the Hadith (the traditions of Muhammad, see page 13). It is often said, "A Muslim lives 10 percent by Qur'an and 90 percent by Sunnah."

# FIVE ASSUMPTIONS HELD BY MUSLIMS

1. Muslims see man as the highest of God's creation, but do not believe that man is made in God's image.
2. Man cannot be sure of his eternal destiny. Therefore, he must work to improve his chances of entering paradise.
3. Muslims do not believe they need a savior because they are not "sinners" (in the Christian sense). Salvation comes through good works according to the teaching of the Qur'an, based on belief in Allah and that Muhammad is his prophet. Salvation does not come through a personal relationship with God.
4. Muslims believe that their religion is Allah's will for man. The whole world should acknowledge Islam in every area of society.
5. Islam is to be lived according to Shari'ah (Islamic law).

*Shari'ah—Islamic Law*

Since its inception, Islam has been a religion of Ummah (the binding sense of community), and Shari'ah comprehensively governs all aspects of Ummah. As people are born into Islam or convert to it, they are incorporated into the Ummah and are indoctrinated to derive their whole identity from the Ummah.

Contrary to what many people think, relatively few of Islam's legal rules come from the Qur'an, which provides general concepts for the life of the Ummah, but not specific applications.

The Shari'ah gives specific legal directives for the life of the Ummah. The major source for Shari'ah is the Hadith (the traditions of the Prophet), not the Qur'an.

Throughout the world, Muslim communities live under Shari'ah. In some cases Shari'ah is only partially applied. These Muslim communities range from whole nations to small neighborhood communities in America.

The five divisions of Shari'ah include

1. *Adat* (customs)
2. *Mamulat* (labor)
3. *Qud* (contracts)
4. *Ihkam* (legal judgments)
5. *Aqubat* (the penal code)

When fully implemented, the penal code prescribes such penalties as death by beheading for apostasy (leaving Islam), stoning for adultery and chopping off of a hand for theft.

# SUFISM

SUFISM IS REGARDED as a mystical expression of Islam. Sufis themselves regard it as the heart or soul of Islam. The word "Sufi" is derived from the Arabic word *suf*, meaning "wool" because the early Sufis were roughly clothed ascetics. Sufism is considered a means of purifying oneself, or a method of increasing spiritual awareness of the "divine self."

According to Sufism, all Sufis are Muslims, but not all Muslims are Sufis. For them, Shari'ah governs the *conduct* of Muslims, while Sufism (the inner teaching) governs the *thoughts* and *intentions* of Muslims. They teach that we come from Allah and we must return to Allah.

The purpose of life is to rediscover the "real self" and return to Allah. To do this, one must subdue the ego (*nafs*) so that the "divine self" can emerge. Every Sufi disciple must have a Sufi teacher as a spiritual director to guide him in his journey back to Allah. The Sufi teacher must have already experienced the return to Allah.

# THE "DOCTRINE OF ABROGATION" (*NASKH*)

AT TIMES MUHAMMAD said things that he later contradicted or retracted. To explain this, he asserted that Satan had uttered words through his mouth, which were not of Allah. This account is used to justify contradictory statements in the Qur'an. Either the earlier saying was a mistake caused by Satan or was rendered null by some later revelation that takes precedence over it. The early surahs, the Meccan verses, which are of tolerance and respect, have been replaced by the later Medinan verses, which are intolerant and harsh.

Muslims refer to the replacement of these early surahs as abrogation, which simply means that previously revealed truth is no longer true. Muhammad himself argued that the replaced verses are better because they are tied to the power of Allah. Thus, for Muslims it is impossible to have contradictions or apparent contradictions in the text of the Qur'an. They are explained away through abrogation.

The doctrine of abrogation shakes the whole foundation of Muslim theology, and its ultimate result is an arbitrary God. A God who abrogates His word stands in stark contrast to the God of the Judeo-

Christian Bible. The God of the Bible makes covenants and honors them, and He builds upon those covenants with the passing of time: "God's gifts and His call are irrevocable" (Romans 11:29).

## THE "DOCTRINE OF DECEPTION"
### (TAQIYYA or DISSIMULATION)

IN A.D. 622, the Meccan enemies of Islam forced Muhammad and the Muslims to flee to Medina (surahs 75:21-ff, 72:17 & 73:10). As his enemies closed in, Muhammad hid in a cave where a miracle supposedly happened. The cave was covered over with spider webs. Because the cave looked abandoned, Muhammad's pursuers moved on. Thus, Muslims believe that Allah deceived the enemies of the "righteous Muslim cause." This incident led the early Muslims to justify the use of deception for the sake of Islam in dealing with their enemies. In much of the Islamic world today, this "doctrine of deception" is often used in dealings with "unbelievers." Some examples of the applied "doctrine of deception" include:

❖ Robbing caravans
❖ Annexing property
❖ Declaring war
❖ Making "treaties" of convenience that were later broken (Muslims looked at these treaties as mere "truces").

Because the motives of non-Muslims—infidels—are suspect, deception may be necessary in dealing with them.

## THE SPIRIT OF AFRICAN-AMERICAN ISLAM

MUSLIMS IN THE United States, from the Nation of Islam or more orthodox forms of Islam, have their own ideas about America. In particular, however, African-American Islam looks down on the United States of America, and disdains African-American Christians' beliefs and practices.

Members of the Nation of Islam, for example, refuse to join the armed forces, salute the flag, sing the national anthem, or otherwise show respect for the United States. They believe that Black Christians are ignorant and brainwashed. Tension between these two points of view exists in the Islamic African-American communities in relation to both individual and group involvement in the United States and the rest of the world.

In one particular case, a Muslim American *did* join the U.S. military:

> In March 2003, the tens of thousands of U.S. military troops camped out in the Kuwait desert were uneasy. They were poised to invade Iraq, but the date of the invasion still lay in question. They trained, they imagined what war would be like and they waited. There were occasional warnings that incoming Scud missiles, possibly bearing chemical warheads, had been launched toward the encampment. Everyone was on edge.
>
> At 1 A.M. on a Sunday, the elite 101st Airborne Division was suddenly torn apart by exploding grenades. "How did the enemy get into our camp?" asked Bart Womack, a command sergeant major. In the wake of the explosions, which were followed by gunfire, Army Capt. Christopher Seifert, twenty-seven, and Air Force Maj. Gregory Stone, forty, were dead. Fourteen other troops were injured.
>
> The "enemy" was neither an Iraqi commando, nor a Middle Eastern terrorist. He was an African American, Hasan Drim Akbar, thirty-one, who was convicted April 21, 2005, by a military jury of murdering two fellow military personnel and injuring fourteen others.
>
> The *Washington Post* reported, "He was born Mark Fidel Kools, but his mother changed his name to Hasan Akbar. He

had risen out of the rough Watts neighborhood of Los Angeles to earn aeronautical and mechanical engineering degrees at the University of California at Davis."

Prosecutors argued that Akbar told investigators he launched the attack on his comrades in the 101st Airborne Division because he was concerned U.S. troops would kill fellow Muslims in Iraq. Akbar seemed to have jihad in mind also, because it was pointed out during his trial that he had written in his diary, with regards to his fellow soldiers that once he was sent to Iraq, "I am going to try and kill as many of them as possible."

"Sgt. Akbar executed that attack with a cool mind," prosecutor Capt. Robert McGovern said during closing arguments, cocking Akbar's unloaded M-4 rifle and pulling the trigger twice for emphasis. "He sought maximum carnage." Akbar has been sentenced to death.

## Chapter Two Discussion Questions:

1. Muslims believe that obedience to Allah through the Five Pillars of Islam is the way to salvation. Christians believe that redemption from sin and salvation into eternal life comes as the result of faith, not works. However, James 2:26 says, "As the body without the spirit is dead, so faith without deeds is dead." How does this passage differ from Muslim belief?

2. Islam does not teach that man is made in God's image; Christians and Jews do believe this (Genesis 1:26). What differences in behavior might result from these conflicting beliefs? If we believe that all human beings are made in God's image, how will that affect the way we treat them?

3. Muhammad died in A.D. 632 without leaving a written record of his recitations. His followers had memorized parts of what he had said, and that was later written down—this

is what is called the Qur'an. How does this method of recording Allah's Word differ from the way the Old and New Testaments came into existence?

4. Discuss why the Muslim belief in abrogation leads to confusion and contradiction in interpreting the Qur'an. Do Christians believe that Satan could have played a part in the writing of Christian scriptures? Why? Why not?

5. Muslims believe that the Ummah, or Islamic community, is greater than any nation, and some radicals are working toward a pan-Islamic empire that will reach all around the world. Christians also believe that the Body of Christ—meaning all believers—is a community that transcends national borders. Yet these beliefs can lead to very different actions. Why? Read Romans 13:1-7 and discuss how it differs from the beliefs and actions of radical Islamic movements.

# 3

## PROTECTING OUR CHURCHES

As we've seen, Islam is actively pursuing African-American children and youth. This is happening throughout the United States. The first thing we must do to protect our churches and communities from Islam is to learn everything we can about Muslims. We can do this by setting aside time to read and study carefully the basic outline of Islamic beliefs and practice.

To make this easier, we have put many of the basics together for you in the book you're reading. For additional information, we have provided a list of other books and resources at the back of this book. This information will help you better understand the spiritual deception and dangers of Islam, will assist you in protecting those who are at risk for conversion and will show you how to talk to Muslims about Christianity.

As you study, here are some suggestions from Dr. Don Davis, director of World Impact's Urban Ministry Institute, that will be of great help to you.

## RECOGNIZE ISLAM'S STRATEGY

ISLAM CLAIMS TO offer African Americans three important things:

1. A sense of dignity

2. A sense of identity
3. A sense of personal security and significance

*A sense of dignity* comes through practices involving self-discipline, along with a new sense of belonging to a purposeful community with a clear sense of direction and history. Islam attracts Blacks by offering a dignity they may not have experienced before.

Islam also offers African Americans *a sense of identity*. By connecting the life struggles of African Americans to a keen sense of history, ethnic integrity and personal responsibility, Islam has given many African Americans an alternative to an Americanized Christianity oriented to the dominant culture—one which either ignores altogether the critical life concerns of the Black community or, on the other hand, sides with policies and practices that limit rather than expand African-American hopes and opportunities.

And Islam offers African Americans *a sense of personal security and significance*. By embracing clear and dignified roles for men, women and children in family, community and society, African-American Muslims have found a sense of belonging and security that they have not felt in their traditional commitment to Christian religion. Unfortunately, "Christianity" as practiced in America has too often hindered this sense of belonging and significance by mirroring the narrow and bigoted policies of America's dominate culture in its own practices and conduct.

The dignity, identity, security and significance offered by Islam may temporarily meet needs in individual lives. But in reality, they are counterfeits of the good and perfect gifts God provides for His people through His Son Jesus Christ. When Christ's Gospel is lived authentically through His body, the Church, and reaches out to the community as it should, our young people will not be vulnerable to empty promises of dignity, identity and significance through anyone or anything other than Jesus Christ Himself.

Meanwhile, since the 1970s, another set of core cultural issues has emerged that Islam (especially Louis Farrakhan) claims to address: pain, rage and a quest for true manhood. ("Gangsta rap" is the voice of this search for masculinity, and machismo the supposed resolution.) In the minds of many young African Americans, these three issues seem more important than dignity, identity, security and significance.

## LEARN ABOUT THE SIGNIFICANCE OF CHRISTIANITY TO BLACK HISTORY

THINK ABOUT THESE three questions:

1. Does "Black life" in and of itself matter in the modern world?
2. Does the presence of Blacks in the Bible make a difference to us today?
3. Are these questions important to identifying and addressing critical concerns in the Black community?

The answer to all three questions, of course, is yes. These background questions are key to presenting the Gospel to African Americans (see Chapter 5).

## CONCENTRATE ON ENCOURAGING AND RECLAIMING YOUNG PEOPLE

As we are seeing, the fastest growing segments among African Americans who resonate with the overall messages of Nation of Islam faith and practice are young people, especially those associated with the Black urban poor culture. Many rappers boast of their allegiance to the Nation or other forms of radicalized Black Muslim ideology, and through their music make its message appealing to new generations of Black and young urbanites.

While this interest in Islam balloons, so interest in the Church and its message appears to wane. Why? Because we have either tended to abandon the young or thrown up our hands in frustration towards them. A key component of our response to the Islamic challenge must take seriously our need to reclaim, encourage and equip our young people in the name of Christ.

Try to talk to the young people you know and help them explore how the issues of identity, dignity and significance—as well as pain, rage and a quest for true manhood—are being played out in the urban "hip-hop" generation. Talk openly with them about the emerging peril of the Islamic challenge, and teach them the blessings and responsibilities in knowing Christ.

## HELP ESTABLISH STRONG MALE LEADERSHIP

DO WHAT YOU can to make sure there is godly male leadership in your congregation and the community.

With some estimates as high as 75 percent female membership in the African-American Church, it is easy to see how the Islamic focus on *male* leadership might appeal to African-American young men, who are too often fatherless and without male role models. Use the Bible to counter the widespread misunderstanding that Christian faith either emasculates its men (on the one hand) or belittles its women (on the other).

Rediscover the Bible's plan for the family, and speak frankly about present challenges to the Black family—the high percentage of out of wedlock births, ever growing numbers of fractured and broken families and lack of male leadership in a high percentage of African-American homes.

# PRAY FOR AND MINISTER TO PRISONERS AND THEIR WIVES AND FAMILIES

CHARLES COLSON WRITES in *First Things* (November 2002):

In the U.S., just two weeks after the September 11 attacks, Muslim Chaplain Aminah Akbarin at New York's Albion Correctional Facility was put on paid administrative leave after telling inmates that Usama bin Laden should be hailed as "a hero to all Muslims" and that the terror attacks were the fault of President Bush. . . .

Radical imams are not the only problem. I recently spoke with an Islamic leader who said he was not as concerned about the imams as he was about hotheaded inmates who convert to Islam. With no one to moderate them, he said, "they could become dangerous."

This news should surprise no one. Muhammad, after all, wrote the teachings of Islam in the middle of a war. We can appreciate that most Muslims view jihad as simply an internal struggle, but we cannot fault those who read the Koran literally—especially if they convert behind bars.

Consider: You're Black, and you believe you're being oppressed by the White power structure. Along comes a person of color who invites you to join the brotherhood—the most appealing aspect of Islam in prisons—and offers you a means of striking back at your oppressors. If, on top of that, prisoners are taught that the more aggressive they are, the more favor they gain with Allah, you have a dangerous mix.

JOE AVILA OF Prison Fellowship writes:

> James (this name and others used are fictitious) was ex-military and a second-time offender in my cellblock. We shared the same work detail and attended some classes together. James hated all White men and referred to all non-Islamic people as infidels. He was always angry or silent and preferred being called by his Islamic name, Malik. His plan upon release was to be smarter and not get caught by "the White man," and to take as much as he could. I can only imagine where James is now.
>
> Tony was much younger than James when I met him and much more naïve. He was a Christian and we spent a lot of time in chapel together. Other African-American prisoners always ridiculed Tony and he soon stopped attending chapel. We saw each other daily and soon he informed me that he was attending *masjid* (an Islamic place of worship). I told him I would be praying for him. I remember a few weeks later, he had a big smile on his face because he had just received his Koran. He also told me that he had ordered a prayer rug. I felt we were drifting apart, only because he was no longer a Christian. As time went on we seldom talked and he, too, became serious and angry. He soon took a new name and surrounded himself with other Muslims.
>
> In six years I saw many more men like James and Tony and by then I had formed my opinion: When young African American men go to a prison where there are radical Islamists, they are actively recruited to Islam (recruited, in our nation's prisons, at the rate of about thirty thousand per year). They have the option of selecting a new name, which gives them, in a sense, a new identity. They get to keep their anger at the establishment for sending them to prison because they are led to believe that they are an oppressed people. Forgiveness and reconciliation are not options. . . .

We must be concerned about these men who get converted in prison and embraced by a radical mosque upon their release. A true religion of peace would not let anyone harbor resentment and hate but rather offer an avenue of reconciliation and restoration.

CHARLES COLSON REVISITED this issue in a September 2006 *BreakPoint* article:

I don't usually make predictions, but here's one I'll venture: If, God forbid, an attack by home-grown Islamist radicals occurs on American soil, many, if not most, of the perpetrators will have converted to Islam while in prison.

I am hardly going out on a limb here. I said this first in 2001. The spread of an especially virulent form of Islam within American prisons is obvious to those of us who have spent time in these prisons. It's the rest of American society that is in denial. Now, thanks to a new study, ignorance is no longer an option.

The study, titled "Out of the Shadows," concluded that "the U.S. . . . is at risk of facing the sort of homegrown terrorism currently plaguing other countries." The source of that risk, according to researchers from George Washington University and the University of Virginia, is "[America's] large prison population."

"Radicalized prisoners" within this population "are a potential pool of recruits by terrorist groups," the study says. The sources of radicalization are incarcerated Islamic extremists and outside organizations that support them. The report notes that the absence of "monitoring by authoritative Islamic chaplains" permits "materials that advocate violence [to infiltrate] the prison system undetected."

Some of this material is provided by known al-Qaeda affiliates. It "[urges Muslim prisoners] to wage war against non-Muslims who have not submitted to Islamic rule." As a former employee of a radical Islamist group who is now a Christian told a Senate committee, "I know of only a few instances in which prisons rejected the literature we attempted to distribute—and it was never because of the literature's radicalism."

OUR AMERICAN PRISONS are on the front lines in the battle for our sons' souls. As we've seen, the number of prison conversions to Islam is dramatically higher than the number of prison conversions to Christianity. Here are some suggestions for you and your Christian community:

❖ Reach out to inmates and their spouses and loved ones, who have likely been exposed to Islamic belief and practice in prison and may be especially vulnerable to similar appeals from Muslim contacts outside.

❖ Prayerfully consider and explore ways that your church can become available to serve these inmates and their families.

❖ Make every effort to befriend and influence the vulnerable men who are behind bars, keeping in mind the high numbers of African-American men who are embracing the Islamic appeals in prison.

❖ Talk to your chaplain at the local jail or the prison in your area to discover ways you and your church might connect with other ministries (such as Prison Fellowship) that reach out to prisoners.

❖ Seek to create a welcoming, loving atmosphere in your church, one that will allow you to incorporate released inmates and their families into your congregation with honor and care.

Carl Ellis writes:

I began to feel sick as one of the inmates came to the front of the room. When I arrived at the prison to conduct the week-long seminar, I was warned that the group to which this man belonged planned to disrupt everything.

Despite minor incidents during the week, the threatened disruption had not occurred.

So, after my last lecture, I thought it would be safe to ask if anyone wanted to share a testimony with the assembled inmates and community volunteers. This has always been a crucial time in my seminars, especially for non-Christians. It gives them a chance to sort out what God has been saying to them.

But when Bra'heem got up wearing his *kuffi* (a knitted head covering similar to a skull cap), I thought I had lost the gamble.

"Everyone knows who I am, right?"

The crowd nodded.

He continued. "You all know that I'm Muslim, right?"

Several nodded.

"Well tonight," he said, "I want you all to know that—as a result of this seminar—this is one Muslim who now follows Jesus Christ."

I breathed a sigh of relief.

Bra'heem was not saying he was instantly converted. Rather, he was ready to begin a discipleship process. This breakthrough made me appraise my approach to Muslims. I continued to correspond with him and got him into touch with some Prison Fellowship volunteers. He eventually became a Christian and got involved with a church after his release.

∞

# REFUSE TO DEMONIZE OR DENIGRATE MUSLIMS OR ISLAM

ALTHOUGH WE MAY disagree with many aspects of Islam, we serve no good purpose by speaking rudely or harshly about it to those who embrace it. The opposite is true. Therefore:

❖ Communicate the Word of God with love, understanding and humility.
❖ Do not stereotype, talk trash or otherwise be hostile toward Muslims and their faith.
❖ Affirm, without any hesitation, that all Muslims, like all other human beings, are made in the image of God, and are invited to new life in Jesus Christ.
❖ Refuse, under any circumstances, to misinterpret or falsely accuse their beliefs or treat Islamic faith and practice as if all Muslims feel the same way about all issues.
❖ Reveal to Muslims Christianity's deep belief that they, too, are included in the love of God through Jesus Christ for the world (1 John 2:2).

Every person, regardless of background, nationality or culture, is created by God and endowed with the honor and dignity intrinsic to human beings. We honor Muslims as people for they are God's precious creation, deserving of our protection, love and respect

This necessity to love, and to avoid the stereotyping of Islamic faith and practice, does not, however, mean that we ought to use kid gloves when we talk about their beliefs. We must be direct and clear about our faith, and honest and fair in explaining the teachings they observe, even as we relate to them as unique and precious persons before God.

As Christians of conscience, we must engage our Muslim neighbors with clarity, critically and carefully spelling out how our faith differs from their understanding of the world and the spiritual realm. Our compassion and deference should reflect our commitment never to sugarcoat the parts of Islamic faith and practice that seem to suggest the "dark side." To be both *fair* and *critical* is the goal of our dialogue with Muslim faith and practice. As those who believe that the God and Father of our Lord Jesus *is* God, and that Jesus Christ His Son *is* Lord, we dare do no less.

## Focus on the Person of Jesus Christ

THE PERSON AND work of Jesus Christ stands at the center of all we do as Christians. Christ is the source and sum of our faith, our hope and our destiny. This is the clear testimony of the scriptures themselves:

Acts 3:20 (ESV) That times of refreshing may come from the presence of the Lord, and that he may send the Christ appointed for you, Jesus.

Acts 5:42 (ESV) And every day, in the temple and from house to house, they did not cease teaching and preaching Jesus as the Christ.

Acts 8:35 (ESV) Then Philip opened his mouth, and beginning with this Scripture he told him the good news about Jesus.

Acts 11:20 (ESV) But there were some of them, men of Cyprus and Cyrene, who on coming to Antioch spoke to the Hellenists also, preaching the Lord Jesus.

1 Cor. 1:23 (ESV) But we preach Christ crucified, a stumbling block to Jews and folly to Gentiles.

2 Cor. 4:5 (ESV) For what we proclaim is not ourselves, but Jesus Christ as Lord, with ourselves as your servants for Jesus' sake.

Eph. 3:8 (ESV) To me, though I am the very least of all the saints, this grace was given, to preach to the Gentiles the unsearchable riches of Christ.

Phil. 1:15-18 (ESV) Some, indeed, preach Christ from envy and rivalry, but others from good will. [16] The latter do it out of love, knowing that I am put here for the defense of the gospel. [17] The former proclaim Christ out of rivalry, not sincerely but thinking to afflict me in my imprisonment. [18] What then? Only that in every way, whether in pretense or in truth, Christ is proclaimed, and in that I rejoice. Yes, and I will rejoice.

1 Tim. 3:16 (ESV) Great indeed, we confess, is the mystery of godliness: He was manifested in the flesh, vindicated by the Spirit, seen by angels, proclaimed among the nations, believed on in the world, taken up in glory.

## ESTABLISH AN EFFECTIVE MINISTRY OF PRAYER FOR MUSLIMS

* Launch any outreach to Muslims with an aggressive and continuous *intercessory ministry* that pleads with God on their behalf and seeks His protection on our behalf.
* Form a prayer ministry or prayer group that focuses on these issues in order to have a great impact on your community, both in understanding and dealing with the Islamic challenge.
* Pray for the illumination of the truth in Muslim circles, especially those who live in your community (remember both imams and members).
* Pray for the Holy Spirit to burden the local Muslim community with a desire to know Christ, with an awareness of the truth among them, and for opportunities and open doors to share the Good News with Muslims in the community.
* Pray that the Lord would make Himself known to these Muslims as He graciously uses your efforts to make Christ real to them, right where they live, work and play.
* Remember that nothing impacts the hearts and minds of unbelievers like concerted and directed prayer.

# INCORPORATE MUSLIM CONVERTS INTO THE CHURCH

❖ See your neighborhood church as an embassy, and see yourself as an ambassador of Christ, exhorting our Muslim friends as God's own agents and representatives to come to God in Christ (2 Cor. 5:20).

❖ Be aware that God's goal is not merely conversion but discipleship, and that all who respond in faith to the Gospel of Jesus Christ should be incorporated into His own body, the Body of Christ.

❖ Welcome with open arms every Muslim who positively responds to the Gospel and become his/her new family and kin. The Biblical testimony bears this out:

> Rom. 15:5-7 (ESV): May the God of endurance and encouragement grant you to live in such harmony with one another, in accord with Christ Jesus, [6] that together you may with one voice glorify the God and Father of our Lord Jesus Christ. [7] Therefore welcome one another as Christ has welcomed you, for the glory of God.

> Matt. 18:10 (ESV): See that you do not despise one of these little ones. For I tell you that in heaven their angels always see the face of my Father who is in heaven.

> 1 John 4:7-11 (ESV): Beloved, let us love one another, for love is from God, and whoever loves has been born of God and knows God. [8] Anyone who does not love does not know God, because God is love. [9] In this the love of God was made manifest among us, that God sent his only Son into the world, so that we might live through him. [10] In this is love, not that we have loved God but that he loved us and sent his Son to be the propitiation for our sins. [11] Beloved, if God so loved us, we also ought to love one another.

Matt. 25:40 (ESV): And the King will answer them, "Truly, I say to you, as you did it to one of the least of these my brothers, you did it to me."

John 13:34-35 (ESV): A new commandment I give to you, that you love one another: just as I have loved you, you also are to love one another. [35] By this all people will know that you are my disciples, if you have love for one another.

*If you are a pastor, Christian leader or teacher, here are some ideas you may be able to use:*

# PREPARE

FIND BOOKS, TRACTS and pamphlets that have been specially designed to handle all of the thorny issues ex-Muslims will need to understand upon entering the church. Ask your pastor about having a special Sunday school or membership class where time is given to address these issues.

# ADDRESS THE ISLAMIC CHALLENGE

IN ORDER TO help your congregation grow in its understanding of Islam, you might want to dedicate some of your preaching and teaching sessions to deal with the rising Islamic presence in urban America. And as you lay out your preaching and teaching schedule for the upcoming year, prayerfully consider how you might commit time to address from your pulpit or teaching platform the rising challenge of Islam in your community.

You could sponsor a Sunday school class or workshop in your church, or maybe preach a series focusing on the challenge of Islam. You may want to host a church-wide emphasis weekend or week on the need for your congregation to be aware of and respond to the challenge of Islam today. And if you don't believe you have the time or resources to do a thorough job yourself, you might even consider scheduling a seminar taught by experts on the subject.

## CREATE YOUR OWN WORKING OUTLINE ON ISLAM

REGARDING YOUR OWN preparation, make certain that you create a *basic outline of the beliefs and practices of Islam.* Your own outline should be concise and reproducible. Keep its structure *basic* by concentrating on the central ideas of Islamic faith and practice (the first two chapters of this book may be helpful).

Also, as you study and discuss the various elements of Islamic faith and practice, make sure that your outline is *fair.* In other words, do not caricature or misrepresent Islamic dogma for the sake of argument. Make sure that your summary of their ideas fairly portrays what they believe and do.

Finally, keep your outline *simple and clear.* Your studies should highlight the critical areas of their faith and practice (e.g., the Five Pillars of Islam). The goal is not for you to become an expert about Islamic faith and practice. All you have to do is accurately represent and summarize their most critical and significant doctrines and practices.

## CLEARLY COMMUNICATE THE NATURE OF THE ISLAMIC CHALLENGE

AS YOU OPEN this conversation and dialogue about Islam with your congregation or class, clearly emphasize the aggressive nature of the Islamic mission *(da'wa).* In other words, you must convince your people of the serious challenge that Islam poses for Christian faith in urban America. Carefully inform your congregation that Islam is expanding rapidly in America, especially among African Americans and young men in prison. Those of us who are urban believers in Jesus Christ need to become more concerned about this ever-growing influence by highlighting Islam's dynamic urban appeal, especially among the Black poor.

## INSTRUCT YOUR CONGREGATION ON THE STRATEGIES OF ISLAM

WHILE WE ACKNOWLEDGE the apparent benefits to some Black families who have joined the ranks of Islam in America, we must also equally acknowledge the power of the Gospel of Jesus Christ to transform the personal lives and address the critical concerns of African Americans who embrace it. We must help our congregants understand just how allegiance to Jesus Christ and His Kingdom more effectively and clearly answers their core concerns for dignity, identity, security and significance, as well as pain, rage and the quest for true manhood.

The Word of God is clear regarding God's commitment to the poor, the widow, the orphan, and the oppressed. As pastors of the Church, it is our responsibility to help our congregations understand how thoroughgoing the Holy Scriptures are in addressing these central issues of injustice, oppression and social righteousness. We must enable our people to find practical ways to serve and meet the real needs of those who live within our communities. This is our job and our task.

## BE AN OUTPOST OF THE KINGDOM OF GOD IN YOUR NEIGHBORHOOD

THE APPEAL OF Islam among the Black poor is directly related to its ability to identify and solve the very real problems of security, safety, meaning and social problems faced by the Black community. In other words, deeds of charity and service engender within the members of the Black community a confidence that the Muslims are legitimate—not because of their words but because of their deeds. Their actions of advocacy and care for the real needs of people in the community give them tremendous credibility, especially when those needs aren't being met effectively by the Church. Muslims have the edge with men because they are perceived as the only ones addressing dignity, identity, security, significance, pain, rage and the quest for true manhood. Men—our sons—are more oriented to these issues.

This attention to social need has been and continues to be a hallmark in all effective Kingdom advancement. Jesus and the apostles make plain that the true sign of authentic discipleship is real love, demonstrated in actual care to others (cf. John 13:34-35; 1 John 4:7-8; James 2:14-26). One of the great tragedies of many congregations today is that they have allowed their concerns for health and wealth to eclipse their duty to demonstrate practically the love of Jesus to their neighbors.

Every urban congregation must re-embrace this fundamental call to be the hands and feet of Jesus in the communities where they live and worship. The challenge of Matt. 5:14-16 is still in effect to the urban church: we are to so let our lights shine that men and women may *see our good works* and so glorify God the Father above (cf. also Eph. 2:10). We are called to be a community where the freedom, wholeness and justice of the Kingdom of God is celebrated, demonstrated and advocated in all our works and actions.

## EQUIP YOUR MEMBERS TO SHARE THE GOSPEL WITH MUSLIMS

ONCE YOU LEARN the tenets of Islamic belief and practice, and are beginning to protect your flock from Islam's onslaught within the community, also seek to train each member of your congregation to share their personal testimony and the Gospel. Muslims are God's creation, people for whom Christ lived, died and rose again. He wants to win them to Himself. He longs to deliver them from the tyranny of "works" (righteousness without assurance of acceptance), into the glorious freedom of Jesus Christ.

It is clear that we are to provide our Muslim neighbors with a clear and persuasive presentation and demonstration of the Good News of Christ, and to do so humbly and with integrity. Peter's exhortation is still appropriate for us today: "But in your hearts regard Christ the Lord as holy, always being prepared to make a defense to anyone who asks you for a reason for the hope that is in you; yet do it with gentleness and respect, having a good conscience, so that, when you are slandered, those who revile your good behavior in Christ may be put to shame" (1 Peter 3:15-16 [ESV]).

In some cases, the best possible (and fastest!) way to win Muslims to Christ is to plant a church among a Muslim population. Because the barriers are so strong, it may be necessary for us to consider the possibility of *launching church planting efforts among Muslim populations* in your vicinity. Church planting is a proven and effective method of incorporating Muslim converts into a church setting that resonates with their lifestyle and culture. Announcing the Good News of Jesus Christ among differing cultures is the hallmark of missions, and a wonderful way of ensuring that the new converts are welcomed and cared for in a setting where their freedom in Christ can be recognized and celebrated.

God may lead some of our congregations to consider establishing sister fellowships where worship styles, leadership processes and cultural norms become *more culturally conducive to Muslim converts* than our traditional congregational styles. In either case, we must strive in every way not merely to announce the Good News to our Muslim neighbors, but also to guarantee their entrance and welcome into the Body of Christ once they believe in Christ for their salvation. Discipleship, not conversion alone, is the goal of all authentic urban ministry to Muslims.

### Chapter Three Discussion Questions:

1. Why are a sense of dignity, a sense of identity and a sense of personal security and significance important to young African-American males? In what way does true Christianity offer these qualities to all believers?

2. One of the reasons Islam appeals to young Black men is because of its male dominant, patriarchal social structure. Christianity was founded primarily by strong, courageous men. How does today's African-American Christian community differ from that of the early Church? What can be done to strengthen a sense of male dignity, identity and significance in today's African-American churches?

3. People often say "the pen is mightier than the sword," and this is certainly true of God's Word. But what about prayer? Do you believe that focused prayer for the salvation of Muslims is a mighty weapon, important to your community? Read Ephesians 6: 10-18. How might this passage apply to Christians who confront Islam?

4. Many Christians who do evangelistic work among Muslims say that introducing the Person of Jesus Christ is a far better approach than debating the differences between Islam and Christianity. Do you agree or disagree with this idea? Why?

5. What do you think is the most challenging aspect of reaching out to Muslims with the Christian Gospel? What do you most fear? What gives you the most hope when you think about this kind of outreach?

# 4

---

# HOW ISLAM DEVELOPED IN THE
# AFRICAN-AMERICAN COMMUNITY

---

IT BEARS REPEATING: before we can respond to Islam, we need
to understand it as well as possible. In the early pages of this book
we have learned about some of the origins and practices of orthodox Islam. Bear in mind that there are many differences between such
Islamic groups as Sunnis, Shi'ites and Sufis and the American movements like Nation of Islam and its many offshoots.

Before we look at American versions of Islam, let's take a moment
to think about how Christian theology developed in Black America.
In many ways, the collapse of that theology opened the way for Islam.

It wasn't long after the slaves discovered Christianity in the South
that *a theology of suffering* developed, addressing several core issues
related to salvation. Among the slaves, the church was seen as a
haven, a place where they did not have to deal with the suffering that
so dominated the rest of their lives.

## THEOLOGY OF SUFFERING

THE THEOLOGY OF suffering was presented through the Bible story
of the Hebrew Exodus. We've all heard the themes of deliverance from

slavery and oppression many times reflected in the spiritual music of the slaves: "Deep river, I want to cross over Jordan. Deep river, I want to cross over to campground." Or the classic, "Go down Moses. Way down in Egypt land. Tell ol' Pharaoh to let my people go."

While the southern theology of suffering encompassed personal and social issues, for our purposes, I want to focus on three core cultural issues:

* Survival
* Refuge
* Resistance to oppression

*Survival* was the first core cultural issue addressed by the theology of suffering. Obviously, the slaves found themselves in a dangerous situation. As a result, survival was a critical issue for them.

*Refuge* was the second important issue. The church was seen as a place where they could escape, to some extent and, for a time, the domination of their White slave masters. Interestingly, the masters thought that being allowed to have church pacified slaves. But the slaves outsmarted their masters by developing a way of worshiping and communicating through double entendre, or double meanings. They made it appear that they were going along with the slave masters' false Christianity, but, in fact, they weren't.

*Resistance to oppression* was the third core cultural issue addressed by the theology of suffering. The institution of slavery was so overwhelming that it was virtually impossible to resist it completely. However, many of the slaves began to resist it physically by having church all Sunday, and to resist it through oral tradition and song.

Negro spirituals were the first expression of a distinct African-American theology. This form of oral tradition and its double meaning was an important form of communication. Even today we recognize that the old spiritual songs contained both a theological meaning and a message of freedom.

## THEOLOGY OF EMPOWERMENT

TIRED OF LIVING with abuse and injustice under a theology of suffering, African Americans in the North developed a *theology of empowerment*. This, too, was based on biblical truth, but it relied on different Bible stories—those of the Hebrew Exile. It was in the North that African Americans began to understand that, like the people of Judah, we were exiled from our homeland. It was in the North that people began to talk about the "African Diaspora" and draw a parallel to the Jewish Diaspora—lasting from the time of the fall of Jerusalem to their return there under Zerubbabel (see Ezekiel 4:1, 24:27; Haggai 1:12, 2:23).

Like the southern theology of suffering, the northern theology of empowerment addressed personal and social issues through salvation by grace through faith in Christ. It also addressed three cultural issues:

❖ Human dignity
❖ African identity
❖ Divine significance of the African-American experience

Human dignity was important for African Americans both in the North and the South, but it expressed itself in different ways. In the South it involved the pursuit of freedom. In the North it involved preserving a positive self-image.

Every day, African Americans in the North were confronted by thousands of messages saying they were abnormal, subhuman, and insinuating that something was wrong with them. This created "the only sin is in my skin" kind of mentality. In response, the northern theology of empowerment promoted the understanding that we, as human beings, were created in the image of God. This truth is a critically important aspect in understanding human dignity.

We generally associate the search for African identity with the Black Consciousness Movement of the late 1960s and early '70s.

However, this movement was based on fundamental concepts that were laid down earlier in the northern theology of empowerment. For example, in the eighteenth and nineteenth centuries, we generally were referred to as "negroes." Yet most of our early institutions were identified by the word "African."

Among the early congregations founded under Black leadership was the African Baptist Church in Savannah, Georgia. The first Black Presbyterian church was founded in Philadelphia, and was called the First African Presbyterian Church. The second was called the Second African Presbyterian Church. The first Black denomination was called the African Methodist Episcopal Church. The second was called the African Methodist Episcopal Zion Church. Among the first Black para-church organizations was the Free Africa Society. Others followed.

African identity was clearly an important issue. Why was it important? It wasn't because African Americans thought that Africa was the perfect place. This identity was an application of Romans 12:2, "Do not conform any longer to the pattern of this world, but be transformed by the renewing of your mind. Then you will be able to test and approve what God's will is—his good, pleasing and perfect will" (NIV).

The northern Black church knew the dominant culture had tagged us as Negroes. They knew that whenever you allow others to label you, you also allow them to define you. Therefore, they said, "We are not going to accept what the larger culture is calling us or how they're trying to define us. No, God did not create us as Negroes. He created us as Africans. And we are going to affirm what God created us to be." The African identity was, in essence, a subtle form of protest.

If you look at this concept a little closer, you discover this response was an early form of Afrocentrism. Although many people don't realize it, Afrocentrism was originally a Christian concept.

The issue of the divine significance of the African-American experience can be summed up in the question: why are we here? It is obvious that African Americans were not immigrants. Immigrants never ask this question because they know why they have chosen to come here. But our ancestors had no choice. They were brought to a foreign country against their will.

In an attempt to discover meaning and gain understanding, Black Christian thinkers asked, "Is there a divine reason why we are here?" They went to the Scriptures to see if anybody else had ever been through a similar experience. They saw that:

- Joseph found himself in Egypt after being sold into slavery (Genesis 37:28). We know from the biblical text that his presence in Egypt had divine and global significance (Genesis 42:6).
- Daniel, Shadrach, Meshach and Abednego were in a similar situation (Daniel 1:6-7). They found themselves in Babylonian captivity, not of their choosing. Yet when we read their story, we see that their presence in Babylon had divine and global significance (3:14-30, 4:3-37).
- Queen Esther lived under The Persians. Her royal position in Persia had divine and global significance (Esther 4:14).

In light of these biblical stories, the African-American presence in America must also have divine and global significance. As Black thinkers wrestled with this truth, they began to sense a call from God to take the Gospel of Jesus Christ to the rest of the African Diaspora and beyond. This diaspora would include people of African descent in Canada, South America, Central America, the Caribbean and throughout Africa.

By 1870, the African-American Church was experiencing explosive growth because core cultural issues were being addressed theologically. In fact, this was one of the most dramatic times of growth in the history of the Church. By the late 1800s, there was an extensive African-American missions movement in Africa. So there was the answer: preaching the Gospel to the rest of the world was an important aspect of the divine and global significance of the African-American experience.

Before the Civil War, as other northern Black Christian thinkers began to affirm a strong kinship with all people of African descent, the Pan-African movement took root. It helped to inspire the founding of the Free Africa Society and continued as interest in African identity increased. As a major force in the 1840s and '50s, this movement helped to shape the theology and early concept of missions in the African-American Church.

This form of Pan-Africanism is in contrast to the form that later emerged during the Black Consciousness Movement. This later movement had a radically different foundation and philosophy, with roots in secular humanism and Marxism. Consequently, many people today fail to realize that Pan-Africanism was, like Afrocentrism, originally a Christian concept.

## A THEOLOGICAL VACUUM

THE AMERICAN INDUSTRIAL Revolution in the North brought massive European immigration and the rise of "White only" labor unions. As a result, African Americans suffered an increasing inability to become part of the "melting pot" and participate in the land of opportunity. In the North, a new kind of racism emerged—institutional racism. As a result, African Americans were excluded from the skilled labor force and mainstream American life. Here marginalization, rather than slavery, became the central problem.

The northern theology of empowerment would have been the ideal basis for the twentieth-century African-American Church to challenge institutional racism and transform its resulting ghetto situation. However, this theology did not survive beyond the close of the nineteenth century. Thus, a theological vacuum developed regarding empowerment and its related issues. By 1910, the explosive growth of the African-American Church had ended.

As the theological vacuum intensified and the successful mission of the Northern Black church dwindled, a new movement began. This one, however, was not based on Christian scholarship. Instead,

the seeds of Islam in America were planted though a curious com-
bination of cult and culture, beginning with the Moorish Science
Temple Divine and National Movement of North America. Most of
the African-American Islamic groups can directly or indirectly trace
their roots back to this sect.

ALTHOUGH NATION OF Islam is the most well known American
Muslim sect today, it is a relatively small movement. The notoriety of
its leader, Louis Farrakhan, as a champion of American Blacks does not
reflect his actual number of followers. Meanwhile, although there are
recent signs of rapprochement between American Sunnis and the
Nation, most Black sects that identify with Islam, including Nation of
Islam, are viewed as heretical in the eyes of orthodox or mainstream
Muslims. This is due to a number of eccentric beliefs, but most notably
because the leaders of these sects usually identify themselves as prophets.
Muhammad is believed by mainstream Muslims to be the final true
Prophet of Allah. Also, these groups are often marred by splits and
schisms, and ultimately lose many of their followers to orthodox Islam.

The first American Muslim sect was the Moorish Science Temple
Divine and National Movement of North America, founded in 1913
in Newark, New Jersey, by Timothy Drew. Drew later became known
as Noble Drew Ali. In 1925, the name of the sect was changed to the
Moorish Temple of Science. Drew Ali claimed that Allah had
ordained him as His prophet to the dark people of America—a
prophet after the order of Jesus, Muhammad, Buddha and Confu-
cius. Ali taught the following:

- ❖ American Negroes were originally from Morocco.
- ❖ North America was originally part of Africa and therefore
  rightfully belongs to Africans.
- ❖ God is tied to a nation and individuals need a national identity before they can have a God or religion.

- ❖ Because the original nation of American Negroes was Morocco, they were originally Moors.
- ❖ The original God of American Negroes was Allah.
- ❖ The original religion of American Negroes was Muslimism.
- ❖ Salvation was found by discovering our national origin and refusing to be called Negro, Black, Colored, Ethiopian, etc.

# Sheik Timothy Givins El and W. D. Fard

Sheik Timothy Givins El was a close disciple of Noble Drew Ali who inherited Ali's mantle of leadership over the Moorish Temple of Science. He established his headquarters in Chicago, Illinois. In 1975, Grand Sheik Richardson Dingle-El founded a splinter group and reverted to the original name, Moorish Science Temple Divine and National Movement of North America.

Wali D. Fard, also known as Wali Fard Muhammad, was a mysterious man who claimed to be from Muhammad's tribe, the Quraish. Fard established his headquarters in Detroit, Michigan. He founded a group called the Temple of Islam.

There is some question as to whether or not Fard was a "card carrying member" of the Moorish Temple of Science. However, all sources agree that Fard was quite familiar with Noble Drew Ali and shared many of his views.

Fard appeared in Paradise Valley of Detroit, claiming to be the *Mahdi* (the "divinely guided one" who will appear in the last days) and "the Prophet" (Muhammad). He declared that he was the leader of the Nation of Islam. Fard claimed to have remedies for the social and economic problems facing Americans of African descent, and asserted that he was here to gain freedom, justice and equality for them. Fard's message was essentially this:

- ❖ Christianity is a tool in the hands of the White slave masters to control the minds of Black people.

❖ White people are devils, the embodiment of evil.

❖ The only hope for Black people in America is total separation and self-reliance.

# ROBERT POOLE

FARD FOUNDED THE first temple between 1930 and 1933. He recruited eight thousand followers among Detroit Blacks. He established religious rituals, founded the University of Islam (a grade school), and created the Fruit of Islam (a paramilitary group). As a result of the organization's rapid growth, Fard found it necessary to train several ministers to help him. Among these was an unemployed autoworker named Robert Poole.

The son of a Baptist minister, Poole knew the Bible quite well. Perhaps this is why Fard selected him. Poole's name was eventually changed to Elijah Muhammad, and he became the chief minister of the Temple of Islam and Fard's eventual successor. With the Temple of Islam well organized, Fard was able to retreat into seclusion. This fueled a belief that he was the "hidden imam" or Allah himself.

In 1932, Elijah Muhammad moved to Chicago and founded Temple #2. However, he returned to Detroit to aid Fard who had been imprisoned. Later, Fard joined Elijah Muhammad at Temple #2 in Chicago, but he was soon arrested there as well. Under the pressure of continued conflict with police, Fard eventually withdrew from the organization altogether and mysteriously disappeared.

The remaining ministers divided the Temple of Islam into two factions. One faction believed that Fard was a prophet of Allah. They were led by Abdul Muhammad and kept the name Temple of Islam. The most dominant faction was based in Chicago and led by Elijah Muhammad. It was first called the Lost, Found Nation of Islam in the Wilderness of North America. Later the name was shortened to the Nation of Islam. Elijah Muhammad believed that Fard was

Allah in person. Eventually, Abdul Muhammad's faction was reabsorbed into the Nation of Islam.

## Elijah Muhammad

Elijah Muhammad expounded his doctrines in the book *Message to the Black Man in America*. Fard's disappearance had made his image as a Christ like figure more marketable. And Muhammad used his familiarity with the Scriptures to present Fard as the fulfillment of prophecy. "You must forget about ever seeing the return of Jesus who was here 2,000 years ago. Set your heart on seeing the One that He said would come at the end of the present world's time (the White race's time). He is called the 'Son of Man,' the 'Christ,' the 'Comforter.'" Muhammad argued that Jesus did not know the day or the hour of the coming of the Son of Man (Matthew 24:36). Thus, he could not have been predicting his own return. Muhammad also asserted that Fard was the Mahdi spoken of in the Qur'an.

Elijah Muhammad taught that the ultimate solution to the problems facing the African-American community was in:

1. Total separation from White society
2. Establishing a Black Muslim state somewhere in North America or elsewhere.

Furthermore, Muhammad taught that integration was a hypocritical and deceptive offer. Its intention was to deceive Black people into believing that the opponents of their freedom, justice and equality were now their friends. Muhammad despised the Christian doctrine of loving one's enemies. In fact, he concurred with Fard's hostile view of Christianity. He saw the Black preacher as the greatest impediment to the progress of the Black race.

The truth that "Christianity" had been used to subjugate Black people is undeniable. Although the Quakers opposed slavery early on, staging the first antislavery demonstration in 1688, most White churches either defended slavery, ignored it or were divided over the issue. In light of this history, the teachings of Elijah Muhammad fell upon eager ears. He was preaching to people who were waiting to claim their dignity and self-sufficiency as well as spiritual fulfillment. He convinced them that the answers to their problems were found only in his version of Islam.

## A STRANGE, NEW THEOLOGY

ELIJAH MUHAMMAD'S TEACHINGS were anything but Orthodox Islam. He taught that Allah was a man—a man called W. D. Fard, whom he knew personally. He taught that Black people created and owned the universe and founded the city of Mecca. He also taught that a mad scientist named Yacub created the White race 6,000 years ago.

According to Elijah Muhammad, Yacub was an exile from Mecca. To take revenge on Allah and on those who exiled him and his 59,999 followers to the island of Patmos, he created a race of White devils through crude genetic engineering. After Yacub's death, this devil race returned to Arabia. They began to turn the peaceful society into a hell, torn by quarreling and fighting. They were eventually exiled to Europe and penned in to keep them from spreading.

Muhammad also asserted that there are twenty-four scientists who rule the universe and write a prophetic book of history prior to each 25,000-year period. They predicted that Yacub would create this race of devils—that Allah would punish the Black man by subjecting them to their evil for 6,000 years. According to Elijah Muhammad, those 6,000 years ended in 1914. The Battle of Armageddon between Blacks and Whites, Muslims and Christians, is about to occur.

Elijah Muhammad also taught the following:

* North America is the spiritual wilderness for the Black man.
* He is the "Prophet," not Muhammad (570-632).
* Prayers to Allah are to be directed to Fard—Allah in the flesh.
* Allah's judgment came in 1914 and 144,000 Black men will eventually reign over the earth.

Like orthodox Muslims, Elijah Muhammad prescribed prayer five times a day. The dietary prohibitions of the Nation of Islam included pork and all pork products, lima beans, cabbage, cat fish, shrimp, oysters and fish over fifty pounds lacking scales.

There is far more to the theology of Elijah Muhammad. However, this brief summary is sufficient to reveal its divergence from Orthodox Islam. It is important to note that Elijah Muhammad was preaching to largely uneducated people, unfamiliar with Islam. Just as he twisted passages of the Bible to suit his purposes, he concocted a version of Islam to address what he saw were the needs of Black Americans.

## The Appeal of the Movement

*The Associated Press,* Wednesday, August 31, 2005

LOS ANGELES—The head of a radical Islamic prison gang and three others were indicted Wednesday on federal charges of planning terrorist attacks against U.S. military facilities, the Israeli Consulate and other Los Angeles-area targets.

The four conspired to wage war against the U.S. government through terrorism, and to kill armed service members and murder foreign officials, among other charges, according to the indictment. . . .

Three of the men are American citizens and the other is a legal permanent resident originally from Pakistan.

Named in the indictment were Levar Haley Washington, 25, Gregory Vernon Patterson, 21, Hammad Riaz Samana, 21, and Kevin James, 29.

Prosecutors contend the plot was orchestrated by Washington, Patterson and Samana at the behest of James, an inmate at the California State Prison-Sacramento who founded the radical group Jamiyyat Ul-Islam Is-Saheeh.

According to the indictment, Washington pledged his loyalty to James "until death by martyrdom" and sought to establish a JIS cell outside prison with members with bomb expertise.

Washington, Patterson and Samana—who attended the same Inglewood mosque—allegedly conducted surveillance of military facilities, the Israeli Consulate and synagogues in the Los Angeles area as well as Internet research on Jewish holidays. Law enforcement officials have previously said that the military facilities included National Guard sites, though the indictment does not specify.

U.S. Attorney General Alberto Gonzales, in announcing the charges in Washington, D.C., referred to the London mass transit attacks in July. "Some in this country mistakenly believed it could not happen here. Today we have chilling evidence that it is possible," he said.

The attacks were to be carried out with firearms and other weapons at synagogues during Jewish holidays "to maximize the number of casualties," authorities said. Patterson allegedly bought a .223-caliber rifle in July.

In Los Angeles, authorities said the suspects could have attacked as soon as the Yom Kippur Jewish holiday in October. "Make no mistake about it—we dodged a bullet here, perhaps many bullets," Los Angeles police Chief William Bratton said at a news conference.

"We have a tendency to think of terrorism as (foreign born)," added U.S. Attorney Debra Yang. "And this is a very stark reminder that it can be . . . local and homegrown. . . ."

James—known as Shakyh Shahaab Murshid, among other aliases—founded JIS in 1997 while imprisoned for an attempted-robbery conviction in Los Angeles County, prosecutors said. He preached that the duty of JIS members was to attack enemies of Islam. Washington was paroled in November 2004, around the time authorities say he joined James' group.

James then instructed Washington to recruit five members without felony convictions and train them to conduct covert operations; acquire firearms with silencers; and appoint a group member to help produce remotely activated explosives, prosecutors claim. In December 2007, declaring themselves "servants of Allah," Kevin James and Levar Haley Wilson pleaded guilty to seditious conspiracy charges; Washington also pleaded guilty to a firearm violation.

The FBI recently ordered its agents nationwide to conduct "threat assessments" of inmates who may have become radicalized in prison and could commit extremist violence upon their release. FBI Director Robert Mueller said authorities have found no links between al-Qaida or other foreign terror groups and the alleged plot.

ACCORDING TO AN FBI report, the Nation of Islam had 500,000 members at its height. When Warith Muhammad took over in 1975, the overwhelming majority went along with his transformation of the NOI into a Sunni group. A very small number broke away with Silas Muhammad, Louis Farrakhan and others. The appeal of this new religion was:

1. Its emphasis on Black self-awareness and self-sufficiency
2. The promise that God was on the side of Blacks in their struggle against racial oppression in America

It is interesting to see who responded to Elijah Muhammad's message. In 1961, C. Eric Lincoln's demographic study of the Nation of Islam revealed some startling things:

❖ The members are young; up to 80 percent of a typical congregation is between the ages of seventeen and thirty-five.
❖ The members are predominantly male.
❖ The members are essentially lower class.
❖ The members are predominantly ex-Christian.
❖ The members are almost totally Black Americans.

This alarming trend continues today. Traditionally, the church in the Black community has had difficulty attracting young males. In an article entitled "Why Most Black Men Won't Go to Church," Reverend William Harris writes:

> Many Black males won't go to church because today's church does not address their needs. The Black male needs money, job opportunities, business resources and relevant skills training. . . . The Church collects money, but does little to create opportunities through which he can make more money. Jesus understood the need to feed people before preaching to them. Today's church must likewise set the table for the Black man before asking him to pay to have the dishes done.

Elijah Muhammad's program for economic development played a crucial part in the rapid growth of the Nation of Islam. With the money donated by the members, Muhammad purchased farmland, storefronts, bakeries, apartment buildings and schools. The economic base of the organization grew in proportion to its numerical growth. By owning businesses and land, Elijah Muhammad was able to provide both housing and employment for those of his followers who lacked these basic necessities. Furthermore, the members had the added pride of sharing in the ownership of these various enterprises and of being, to a great extent, independent of the broader society. Employment was most scarce for young Black males, which offers one explanation why they were drawn to the Nation of Islam in such large numbers.

Men were also attracted to the Nation of Islam because of the emphasis placed on male leadership. African-American churches tend to be dominated by women, with one central male figure, the pastor, in the pulpit. As a result, many men did not feel affirmed in the church environment. They saw the pastor as a threat and even a rival. Elijah Muhammad was able to criticize the Black male while affirming his role. He challenged men to take the lead. Unlike the typical Christian church, the Muslim temples attract many more men than women, and men assume the full management of temple affairs. Women are honored and they perform important functions within a defined role.

The role of women consisted of teaching other women and managing the affairs of the home. Ironically, women were also attracted to the Nation of Islam because they appreciated the strength of the men and protective posture they took towards Black women. As C. Eric Lincoln noted in his research, the Nation of Islam appeals to the young, regardless of gender:

> A surprising number of young people are attracted by the Muslims' redefinition of the roles men and women should play in the home and in the religious life of the sect. There is a strong emphasis on the equality of individuals irrespective of sex, but each sex is assigned a role considered proper to it. The trend in our larger society seems to be toward blurring the distinct line between the traditional social roles of men and women. The Muslims, on the other hand, claim to have

restored the women to a place of dignity and respect. . . . Muslim women seem to welcome the security and protection implicit in this arrangement. . . . Children seem to profit most, for among Muslim children, delinquency is unheard of.

Among people who were not accustomed to the security of a strong, nuclear family with well-defined roles, the Nation of Islam provided a welcome structure. The underlying message of the Nation was that the disorder they had experienced up until then was caused by outside forces beyond their control—evil influences they were now to avoid at all costs.

"Muslim women particularly are forbidden contact with either sex of the White race, on the theory that 1) 'no White man has honorable intentions toward any Black women', and 2) White women are 'immoral by nature.' The White women are said to corrupt the minds of Black women, who then try to imitate them by 'displaying their bodies, neglecting their children, and abandoning their men.'"

Just as Adolf Hitler salved the consciences of the Germans by blaming the Jews for all their economic and political woes, Elijah Muhammad found in the White race the source of every ill within the Black community, especially with regard to the family. Thus the causes for the growth of the movement were both economic and psychological.

## A DYNAMIC YOUNG SPOKESMAN

THE GREATEST PERIOD of growth in the Nation of Islam cannot be directly attributed to Elijah Muhammad. In 1948, while serving a prison sentence in Massachusetts, a young man by the name of Malcolm Little became acquainted with the teachings of Elijah Muhammad and was converted to the Nation of Islam. Upon his release from prison, Malcolm Little, a former pimp, drug pusher, armed robber and numbers man, returned to Detroit and began aggressively recruiting for Detroit Temple #1. He received recognition for his efforts from Elijah Muhammad, who changed Malcom Little's name to Malcolm X. "Malcolm 'X' symbolized his original African name, which he never knew, and replaced the slave master's name, Little." (African Americans are the only American ethnic group that bears the names of their slave masters.) It was customary for converts to the Nation of Islam to be given a new name by Elijah Muhammad, and "X" was commonly chosen. However, Malcolm X, with his new name, would soon make both that name and the organization it represented a symbol of freedom for some and fear for others.

Malcolm X frequently visited Elijah Muhammad in his home in Chicago, where they talked for hours. Because of his aggressive recruiting, new ideas and unyielding devotion to Elijah Muhammad, Malcolm was appointed as national spokesman. He crisscrossed North America, sometimes as often as four times a week. From Detroit to Boston to Philadelphia he traveled, establishing new temples. In 1954, Malcolm X moved to New York City, and became minister of Temple #7. In fact, Malcolm X was instrumental in the establishment of most of the temples in North America, and he said he had increased the membership to forty thousand within a few years after he joined the Nation of Islam.

Even today, Malcolm X remains a major figure in the African-American quest for freedom and dignity. He attracted tens of thousands with his emphasis on:

❖ Cultural concerns
❖ Discipline .
❖ Solidarity of the brotherhood
❖ African identity

These factors continue to be a strong draw to young African-American males. They will not go away for the foreseeable future. Nor will the Church make any significant headway among these young men until we address these concerns. The Bible more than adequately addresses these issues and it is time for us to apply God's word to them.

## MALCOLM—ON HIS OWN

WITH HIS PLATFORM as national spokesman, Malcolm X became an international figure. He was a coveted lecturer at universities, mosques and churches throughout the country. He recruited new leaders to the Nation. He even had a profound influence upon Elijah Muhammad's son, Wallace D. Muhammad (also known as Warith D. Muhammad). For some leaders of the movement, however, Malcolm X was developing too quickly and gaining too much prominence. Many began to view him as a threat to Elijah Muhammad's leadership. He frequently made statements that went beyond the teachings of Elijah Muhammad, and was often reprimanded.

The tension reached its apex when Elijah Muhammad was implicated by two of his former secretaries in a paternity suit. Disillusioned, Malcolm X conducted his own investigation into the allegations, and his worst fears were confirmed.

Shortly after that incident, on December 2, 1963, Elijah Muhammad suspended Malcolm X from the Nation for ninety days following a controversial statement made about the assassination of President John F. Kennedy. On March 8, 1964, when it appeared that his suspension would be indefinite, Malcolm X announced his formal break with Elijah Muhammad and the Nation. Because of his sympathies with Malcolm X, Warith D. Muhammad was also suspended from the Nation of Islam.

Malcolm's ideas were radically changed when he went on the Hajj to Mecca. Upon his return, he started two organizations: Muslim Mosque Incorporated (MMI) and the Organization of

Afro-American Unity (OAAU). MMI was based upon the principles of Orthodox Islam. OAAU was an all-Black nonsectarian organization dedicated to creating a Black brotherhood. Under its ideology, Black and White coalitions would be possible. He encouraged Whites to fight racism and was willing to accept aid from White donors.

However, Malcolm's new vision didn't have a chance to take root. On February 21, 1965, Malcolm X was assassinated while speaking to about 500 people in the Audubon Ballroom in New York City.

## A NEW LEADER WITH NEW IDEAS

In 1969, WARITH D. Muhammad returned to the Nation of Islam. His father, Elijah Muhammad, restored him to the ministry in 1974, giving him freedom to preach what he pleased. On February 25, 1975, Elijah Muhammad died of congestive heart failure. The following day, the Nation held its annual Savior's Day Rally in honor of Elijah Muhammad. There they pronounced Warith D. Muhammad as the new leader.

Under the leadership of Warith Muhammad, the former Nation of Islam has become an orthodox community of American Sunni Muslims. From the moment he took over as leader, he sought to align the doctrine of the organization with the Qur'an and to do away with Elijah Muhammad's doctrine of racial separation.

The organization has gone through a series of name changes—Bilallian Community, World Community Al-Islam in the West (WCIW), the American Muslim Mission and finally the Muslim American Society.

When asked where he saw the organization in the year 2000, Imam Muhammad replied, "I hope Muslims will be so comfortable in America that we won't have to introduce any structure or anything, just be American Muslims."

∞

*The Associated Press,* FEBRUARY 3, 2007

PLAINFIELD, Ind.—The Islamic Society of North America, which represents orthodox, mostly immigrant Muslims, will join ailing Nation of Islam leader Louis Farrakhan this weekend in Detroit at what is billed as his final major address.

Imam Siraj Wahhaj, a longtime member of the Islamic Society, said he has accepted Farrakhan's invitation to give a sermon at Friday prayers ahead of the minister's speech on Sunday at Ford Field, the Plainfield-based Islamic Society said.

The Islamic Society's participation is significant because mainstream Muslims have considered the Nation heretical. Among their many differences, the Nation has promoted Black supremacy, while mainstream Islam teaches racial unity. However, in recent years Farrakhan has adopted more orthodox teachings and has tried to build ties with other Muslims.

The 73-year-old Farrakhan was released last month from a hospital after a 12-hour abdominal operation to correct damage caused by treatment for prostate cancer.

### Chapter Four Discussion Questions

1. Compare the Theology of Suffering with the Theology of Empowerment. Which one most closely characterizes the perspective of your Christian community? What are the strengths and weaknesses of each?
2. What do you believe are the primary reasons African Americans began to follow the eccentric leaders and teachings of Islamic groups cited in this chapter? Do you think those same reasons are still relevant in today's Black communities?

3. What "spiritual vacuum" do you think draws today's young men (and women) into various Islamic groups? How can it be remedied?

༈

# 5

## How Should Christians Respond to Islam?

### Righteousness & Unrighteousness

WE HAVE SEEN that while Muslims believe in Allah, Muhammad and the performance of good works as their means of salvation, Christians believe in the redemption provided by Jesus Christ's death on the cross, followed by his resurrection. It is to God, through Christ's intercession, that Christians commit themselves. And through that commitment, good and righteous works follow.

On the other hand, whenever people lack a basic commitment to God, unrighteousness follows. Both righteousness and unrighteousness have to do with a relationship that is best expressed in God's statement, "I will be your God and you will be my people" (Leviticus 26:12; Jeremiah 7:23, 11:4, 30:22). A simple definition of unrighteousness, biblically speaking, is a failure to do right in our relationship with God.

Scripture identifies at least four kinds of unrighteousness. I (Carl Ellis) call them *ungodliness* and *oppression* as expressed in the *individual* dimension and the *institutional* dimension.

Ungodliness happens when a person sins and suffers his or her own consequences.

Oppression happens when a person sins and forces others to suffer the consequences or when a person tries to force his or her sin on others.

Unrighteous behavior is expressed in the individual dimension by face-to-face intentional sin.

Unrighteous behavior is expressed in the institutional dimension through sin that is woven into the structure and social fabric of society. This type of sin does not need the intention or the consciousness of the individual to have an effect on its victims.

By pairing these dimensions, we end up with four manifestations of unrighteousness as illustrated in the figure below.

|  | INDIVIDUAL | INSTITUTIONAL |
| --- | --- | --- |
| UNGODLINESS |  |  |
| OPPRESSION |  |  |

# EXAMPLES OF UNRIGHTEOUS ACTION

❖ Individual Ungodliness

When we lie, cheat or steal, we manifest individual ungodliness, and it can have far-reaching effects. An infamous illustration of this came in the O. J. Simpson trial (January–October 1995). Mark Fuhrman, the lead police detective in the case, testified that he found incriminating evidence on Simpson's property. In the course of the trial, Fuhrman was accused of being a racist. Under cross-examination in this racially charged case, Fuhrman emphatically stated that he was not a racist. Later, the jury heard taped excerpts from a 1988 interview in which Fuhrman was clearly heard referring to African Americans as "niggers." Not only did this discredit Fuhrman's testimony, it severely damaged the prosecution's case.

❖ Individual Oppression

When we harass, bully or ridicule others, we commit acts of individual oppression. As a pastor, I dealt with scores of people whose lives were adversely affected by the abuse their parents inflicted on them. In too many cases, these negative effects were passed down to succeeding generations. The Apostle Paul warns us about parental abuse, "Fathers, do not embitter your children, or they will become discouraged" (Colossians 3:21, NIV). J. B. Phillips translates it, "Don't over correct your children, or they will grow up feeling inferior and frustrated."

❖ Institutional Ungodliness

The activity of the National Gay and Lesbian Task Force is a good example of institutional ungodliness. This is a community of people who have made a lifestyle choice that is immoral. They pursue it as if it is legitimate and insist that the rest of society must agree with them.

❖ Institutional Oppression

The sharecropper system is a clear example of institutional oppression. In the rural south, being a tenant farmer was often the only means of survival. The landowner was the only source of food, clothing, shelter and farming supplies. Thus, sharecroppers had to obtain these things from the landowner on credit, to be paid in full out of the proceeds from the harvest. Typically, the sharecropper kept from one-half to four-fifths of the yield from his cash crops. He received his share from the landowner in a "settling up" at the end of the harvest. The landowner usually inflated the amount he charged his tenants for what he supplied and minimized what he paid them for their cash crops. The state and local laws favored the landowners. The money that the sharecropper made seldom covered his debt

One reason the church has failed to address the cultural issues of our day is because we tend to focus only on individual ungodliness. As a result, when we encounter the institutional oppression that we've experienced for far too long, we have nothing to say about it and we are unable to show how scripture addresses it. If the whole window of unrighteousness represents our responsibility to fulfill Jesus's Great Commission, then we have withdrawn from perhaps three-quarters of it. To affect cultural unrighteousness, we must begin to address every issue we face through scripture.

## COMPONENTS OF RIGHTEOUSNESS

IN MY BOOK, *Free at Last? The Gospel in the African-American Experience,* I describe righteousness as:

The perpetual pursuit of God and his revelation in every area of life, both individually and corporately. It consists of seeking to live by the principles of the kingdom of God—principles that manifest themselves in [biblical values] such as . . . equality, integrity, compassion, grace and love (p. 261).

Godliness consists of doing right by God; it usually involves devotion and piety. Justice consists of doing right by our fellow human beings; it usually involves freeing people from unjust situations and helping them to do the right thing. These righteous behaviors are expressed in the personal dimension by doing right on a one-on-one basis. They are expressed in the social dimension by doing right corporately as a society.

By pairing these dimensions, we end up with four manifestations of righteousness as illustrated in the figure below.

|  | PERSONAL | SOCIAL |
|---|---|---|
| GODLINESS |  |  |
| JUSTICE |  |  |

## EXAMPLES OF RIGHTEOUS ACTION

❖ Personal Godliness

When we "say grace" before we eat or have daily devotions, we demonstrate personal godliness.

❖ Personal Justice

When we participate in activities that free people from bad circumstances or improve the quality of their lives, we demonstrate personal justice. This includes being a mentor to someone who needs the life skills we have, helping the unemployed find gainful employment, developing a fatherly relationship with fatherless children, etc.

❖ Social Godliness

During the mid-1980s, several top musical entertainers responded to a famine in East Africa by producing a hit recording entitled *We Are the World*. The proceeds from the sale of this record went to a special famine relief fund. These artists did not claim to be Christians. Yet, they were motivated by a sense of compassion for others who were less fortunate. This example of social godliness inspired similar efforts by many other countries.

❖ Social Justice

One of the best examples of social justice was the effect the civil rights movement had on this country. While it did not solve all of America's social ills, it had a positive effect on countless millions, both here and abroad.

In the Christian community in America, we inadequately focus righteousness only on personal godliness. If the whole window of righteousness represents the Gospel, then perhaps we have neglected three-quarters of it. While personal godliness or piety is a good thing, it falls far short of the complete righteousness God calls us to be about. Our failure to demonstrate righteousness, especially the areas of personal and social justice, has caused us to have an inadequate and oftentimes irrelevant theology. To exercise a theology that is appropriate and biblical, we must, by God's grace, display all four manifestations of righteousness, namely: personal godliness, personal justice, social godliness, social justice.

Here are a few general observations about the windows of righteousness and unrighteousness. Each pane of these windows is dependent upon the other three panes for support. If one section is removed or broken, the integrity of the whole window is compromised. The removal of each additional pane further degrades the window's integrity, and ultimately the last pane left will be stressed to the breaking point and lost.

Consequently, we, as the Body of Christ, must address all four manifestations of unrighteousness with the Word of God. We must also practice all four manifestations of righteousness by the power of the Holy Spirit. If we limit ourselves to only the scope of personal godliness and individual ungodliness, we will end up failing in the other areas.

# THE RIGHTEOUSNESS OF GOD

GOD IS THE God of righteousness and justice (Psalm 89:14; 116:5). He has compassion and love for people (Psalm 86:15; 1 John 1:10). The righteousness of God, made available to us through faith in Jesus Christ, sets us free from sin. Unlike Islam, in which religious observance is external, Christian righteousness comes through the work of God's grace in our inner lives. It is by God's grace alone that we have the power and the will to demonstrate righteousness and resist unrighteousness. When God is left out, so is His special grace. And without God's grace, we lose the very possibility of both righteousness and true freedom.

The freedom to obey God and the power do what is right in His sight is the ultimate freedom. John 8:36 teaches us "If the Son makes you free, you shall be free indeed" (NIV). Human freedom comes from God. Therefore, as African Americans, our search for liberation is not a search for freedom *from* God, but a search for freedom *in* God. Apart from the pursuit of righteousness, true liberation is not possible.

The pursuit of righteousness must become the top priority of the African-American Christian agenda if we are to become the people God created us to be (Matthew 6:33). When we move forward in this pursuit, we will have the kind of cultural and spiritual revolution we've needed for a long time. It will help us to understand why God has us here in the first place. And it will propel us to take our rightful place in the unfolding purposes of God in the world, especially when it comes to explaining God's grace and His transforming power to Muslims.

# WITNESSING TO MUSLIMS

NASHID QADUR HASSAN (Henry Hennagan) writes:

I came to the Lord in a Bible club started by students from Columbia Bible College in South Carolina. I was eleven years old. These students were especially excited by my conversion. Thanks to the quality of the discipleship I experienced, I grew in the Lord.

By the time I was a senior in high school, I was convinced that I, too, should go to Bible College. It was the obvious choice. After all, it was a Columbia student who discipled me.

I soon discovered, however, that Columbia did not accept Black Americans. This devastated me! It shattered the White student who discipled me also—so much so that he dropped out of school and walked away from his faith. As of this day, he has not returned to the Lord.

A Jamaican student who was involved in my discipleship did manage to graduate. He left this country distressed by the racist posture taken by the college.

How could a school train students to lead others to Christ yet not allow the fruit of their ministry to be trained? How could they accept Black internationals yet reject Black Americans?

Upon graduating from high school, my only thought was to get as far away as I could from Columbia, Columbia Bible College and its phony "Christianity." And I did!!

After a nine-year downward spiral, and returning to Columbia, I walked into a Nation of Islam meeting on Barnwell Street. The speaker stated emphatically that "the White man is the devil" and that "Christianity is his tool to keep Black people down." He supported his case with historical data and current events. I bought it all! I threw myself completely into making the Muslim programs work. I became so extreme that I would not eat white bread or drink white milk. I stuck to it in spite of the inconsistencies I saw. "This plan can work," I kept saying. "You just need the right people."

For nearly three years this continued until the tragic death of a Muslim brother. The trauma of this death arrested my attention. "It should have been me," I thought. The words

"Allahu Akbar" suddenly seemed so empty. "Lord forgive me" welled up from inside. I hadn't just rejected phony Christianity. I had abandoned the Lord. Yet He never abandoned me.

God did forgive me. He also restored me and gave me a burden to reach others caught up in the sin of racism and unforgiveness.

ONE OF THE PLACES where righteousness and unrighteousness stand in stark contrast with one another is in prison. Both Christians and Muslims are hard at work within the American prison system, seeking to convert inmates. Generally speaking, Christian ministries that work in prisons encounter three types of Muslims: those who belong to the Nation of Islam, to the Moorish Science Temple of America or to mainline or Orthodox Islam. When approaching a Muslim in any of these sects, it is helpful to evaluate why that person embraced Islam in the first place. Three considerations are important.

First, he could be attracted by the standards of Islam—the doctrine, theology and teaching. There are, however, two other reasons that need to be considered.

Reason #1: He could be attracted to Islam because of his situation, be it because of intimidation, a sense of cultural displacement or feelings of alienation. In the Muslim prison community, a young man often is given a brotherhood, cultural affirmation and solidarity. This is especially true for African-American inmates, who often face cultural insensitivity from prison officials.

To make matters worse, some well-meaning Christians who try to reach out to Muslims have inadvertently driven them further away with pictures of a blond-haired, blue-eyed Jesus. This not only violates Muslim teachings concerning idolatry, but also presents a Jesus that reinforces the underlying belief held by many African Americans that Christianity is for Whites, while Islam is for Blacks.

Reason #2: He could be attracted to Islam because of his own motivation and goals—his personal desire for godliness. Some prisoners have been deceived by illusions of instant wealth through crime. They feel alienated from God and consequently want to gain God's favor, hoping to purge themselves from the false values that led to their criminal behavior. Therefore, when an inmate is introduced to the Islamic community with its disciplined, rigorous approach to life, he may see it as his best shot at satisfying his desire for righteousness.

## JESUS-IANITY

ONE OF THE great mistakes we tend to make in approaching Muslims is forcing a "Jesus-ianity" concept upon them—getting to the point of the message too fast. I've often heard a Christian tell a Muslim, "Well, Jesus is God." And certainly He is God, but how did Jesus Himself reveal His deity?

The Lord found creative and effective ways to communicate the truth without directly saying it. Observe, for example, how Jesus revealed His identity to the disciples on the road to Emmaus (Luke 24:13-35).

Why is this important? Because to start out by telling a Muslim that "Jesus is God," sounds to his ears like we are deifying a mere man.

From a biblical perspective, we know that the second person in the Godhead became a man in Jesus Christ. This is incarnation, not deification, but this distinction is seldom communicated to a Muslim. Every Muslim needs to understand that God alone is the object of our worship, and that God's decision to become a man in no way diminished His deity.

Instead of simply confronting a Muslim by pitting our doctrine against his, it is more effective to draw him out through conversation. Many Muslims have personal goals and motivations that are essentially biblical. In such cases, we should learn to be sympathetic and supportive. As a result, barriers often break down.

Only after establishing such camaraderie will a discussion concerning the ways of achieving their goals become meaningful. Then the Gospel really does become "good news." The discussion can take several directions. The following dialogues and illustrations demonstrate three basic approaches:

*The Righteousness Approach:*

(Christian) "Isn't God perfectly righteous?"

(Muslim) "Yes, of course."

(C) "Is it true that God tolerates no unrighteousness whatsoever?"

(M) "Yes."

(C) "Isn't God perfectly just?"

(M) "Yes."

(C) "Doesn't God's perfect justice mean that He will punish all unrighteousness?"

(M) "Certainly."

(This is where I gently lower the boom.)

(C) "Are you perfectly righteous?"

(M) "No! And nobody is."

(C) "Since God tolerates no unrighteousness, then God cannot tolerate you."

(M) "Yes, but I'm striving for righteousness."

(C) "But that doesn't change the fact that God doesn't tolerate you because of unrighteousness. It also doesn't change the fact that because God is just, you must also be punished for your unrighteousness up to now."

A Muslim has no real solution to this dilemma. The best answer he can offer is that God forgives. But the Muslim still lacks assurance of this forgiveness.

(M) "If I can't approach God, then you can't either."
(C) "Oh, yes, I can, and I do."
(M) "How?"
(C) "I come to God on the basis of the perfect right-eousness of Jesus Christ."

I then share that God's forgiveness comes through acknowledgment that in Christ alone I can have assurance of it. A Muslim cannot deny the perfect righteousness of Christ because the Qur'an states it clearly (Surah 3:40-41; 19:9). An explanation of justification now begins to make sense.

*The Relationship Approach:*

(C) "How would you describe your relationship with God?"
(M) "I'm a servant of God, responsible to submit to His will."
(C) "Would you also describe yourself as a slave of God?"
(M) "Yes, this is what the Qur'an teaches."
(C) "This is interesting because I am a son of God."

If your Muslim friend knows his doctrine well, this statement might be repulsive to him. To prevent this response, explain that your sonship is based on *adoption*. Then introduce the teachings of Hebrews 3:1-6, comparing Moses, the servant of God, to Christ, the Son of God. Explain that Christian sonship is greater than Islamic servanthood because the son, not the servant, is the one honored in the Father's house.

*The Submission Approach:*

During a stimulating discussion I had with a Muslim, he finally said, "Carl, you're a Muslim, and you don't know it."

"That's not true," I replied. "I know I'm a Muslim." My response caught him completely off guard.

In Arabic, the term *Muslim* means "one who submits," generally understood to mean "one who submits to the will of God." The term *Islam* means "submission" or, in its popular understanding, "submission to the will of God." As a disciple of Jesus Christ, I am in submission to the will of God. This makes me a true Muslim or a practitioner of true Islam. At this point, I usually share Romans 10:1-4.

Although this passage refers to nonbelieving Jews who have "a zeal of God, but not according to knowledge" (Romans 10:2), it could also apply to Muslims. A Muslim, like a first-century Jew, lives under a law of discipline. According to the Bible, however, true Islam is submission to God's way of putting people right, and that way is Jesus Christ. Just as I am a true son of Abraham by the power of Jesus Christ, I can also be considered a true Muslim by the same power. At this point, I sometimes refer back to my righteousness approach (see pg. 79).

# HAVING PATIENCE

OUR APPROACH TO Muslims must be similar to the Apostle Paul's approach to his Jewish brothers. In acknowledging that nonbelieving Jews had zeal for God, Paul went on to say that this zeal was not according to true knowledge. Paul has given us a biblical example of his motivational and situational approach.

In essence, Paul said, "Though they have the right goals and motivations, they have adopted the wrong means for achieving those goals and satisfying those motivations." Many Muslims will admit, in the final analysis, that they can do nothing to earn God's favor, nothing to save themselves—their only hope of salvation is in God alone.

Is not this the essence of the Gospel of our Lord Jesus Christ? God promises His Word will not return void (Isaiah 55:11), and if, by a skillful application of God's Word, a Muslim begins to understand the truths of the Gospel, God will surely honor it. If we simply plant the seed and water it, God will "give the increase." However, we often find ourselves counting on instant salvation and instant decisions. It doesn't work that way. Muslims need time, patience and, most of all, love. Meanwhile, God is faithful.

## SEEKING POWER

WHILE TEACHING A seminar in a Midwestern prison, I talked to Ahmad, an inmate, several times. Only toward the end of the seminar did I begin to understand him. He seemed to be saying, "Brother Carl, I may be a Muslim, but I'm hurting. When I get out of this place, I don't know if I can stay out of crime. Do you have anything to offer me? What is this power you keep talking about? I pray five times a day; I don't eat pork; I keep all the Muslim disciplines. But I just don't seem to have this power. How can I get it?"

The Qur'an's earlier verses endorsed the Bible. Early Muslims were commanded in the Qur'an to respect what the Bible says (Surah 5:50-51; 6:92; 10:37-38, 94; 35:40). And according to Isaiah 64:6, "all of our righteousness is as filthy rags."

Thus, I began to share with Ahmad that subscribing to all these disciplinary procedures—trying to earn God's favor—was futile. But if he would receive God's gift of grace through Jesus Christ and subscribe to a life of discipline as a means of expressing his thanksgiving to God, then he would be in Islamic balance. And having received God's grace through Christ, he would also receive God's power to stay out of crime.

# FINDING RESONANCE

OMAR IS A close friend in a Southern prison who, like me, was profoundly affected by the great struggle of our people during the 1960s and beyond. A special bond quickly developed between us. We have had many discussions about the canonization of scripture and about the nature of Jesus (*Isa* in Arabic) as a prophet. Eventually, he admitted that Jesus is more than a prophet. In the spirit of Christian love, others in the surrounding community have reached out to Omar. Ironically, however, fellow Muslims have not extended a helping hand.

As in the case of so many Muslims in prison, Omar's mother is a devout Christian who prays for him constantly. Indeed, God is beginning to answer her prayers, and I can see clear evidence that God's spirit is drawing Omar to Christ. But how will the church respond to him when he does come to Christ? Will we be sensitive to him? Or will our churches continue to be ill equipped in dealing with those who come to Christ from a Muslim background?

While valid Christian theology can be done on the "intuitive" as well as the "rational" side of intelligence, historic African-American theology has been more intuitive.

Like Omar, many Muslims I meet grew up in the Church. While they have an Islamic veneer rationally, they intuitively have a Christian outlook. If we learn to deal with a Muslim skillfully, on a rational basis, God's Word will resonate with that intuitive Christian core. Often, this will affect him in more ways than he is willing to admit. "As the rain and the snow come down from heaven, and do not return to it without watering the earth and making it bud and flourish, so that it yields seed for the sower and bread for the eater, so is my word that goes out from my mouth: It will not return to me empty, but will accomplish what I desire and achieve the purpose for which I sent it" (Isaiah 55:10-11).

## BEING CULTURALLY CONSISTENT

ON THE DAY of Pentecost, by the power of the Holy Spirit, the Gospel of Jesus Christ was preached and applied in many languages to many cultures. The Gospel is unique in that it is culturally adaptable to any situation without losing its integrity. Anyone can come to Christ, regardless of his culture or language.

In Islam, on the other hand, no language or culture other than Arabic is considered sacred. Thus, in worship and prayer, the non-Arabic culture and language of the Muslim must be left outside the door.

Despite Islam's cultural intolerance, imprisoned Muslims have done a better job than Christians in affirming African-American roots and culture. It's a shame that, for the African American, Muslims are often more effective at being culturally inconsistent than Christians are at being culturally consistent.

It's not too late for the Christian witness to make an impact. By learning how to apply Scripture to the situations, motivations and goals of those attracted to Islam, we can skillfully, lovingly, patiently and wisely communicate the Gospel to Muslims. The response we get will be lasting.

## RESPECTING LIFESTYLE

I MET YUSEF in an eastern city. He, like Omar, was raised in the Church but had become a Muslim. However, through the reasoned and loving witness of a friend, he was led to Christ. I took him out to dinner where we had an intense discussion about reaching other Muslims. As we were ordering dinner I jokingly asked, "Hey bro, are you back on the swine (pork) yet?" He laughed and said, "No man, I keep the discipline for the sake of my ministry to my Islamic brothers." Over dinner he explained how his keeping his disciplined lifestyle and his Arabic name enabled him to make remarkable break-throughs with Muslims (I Corinthians 9:19-22).

As we begin to deal with Muslims more effectively, we need to develop appropriate, alternative "Muslim-friendly" models of the Church. We also need new types of Christians who, like Yusef, will practice their faith in an Islamic lifestyle.

## PRACTICAL SUGGESTIONS FOR MINISTERING TO MUSLIMS AND THOSE WHO ARE CONSIDERING CONVERSION TO ISLAM

A. Be yourself.
B. Try to understand Islamic doctrine from the perspective of Islam.

   Recognize that the Christianity Muhammad encountered was corrupted. For example, Nestorianism was the dominant Christian sect in Arabia. It was characterized by the celibacy of its monks and endless controversies over the nature of Christ and Mary. In the case of Mary, there were heated debates about whether she was the Mother of God or the Mother of Christ. Often, the veneration of Mary overshadowed the emphasis on God the Father and the worship of God the Son.

   Also, very little scripture had been translated into Arabic. In this language vacuum was an abundance of apocryphal stories and other legendary material. The Qur'an reflects these unfortunate misrepresentations of Christianity.
C. Be a good listener.

   Examine the situation that led him to Islam and the goals he is trying to achieve through it.
   + When the motivation and goals are biblical, affirm them.
   + When they are not, lovingly challenge them.
   + Whenever possible, use words according to his defini-tions, not yours.

D. When dealing with Islamic doctrine, do not use the occasion to show him how much you know about his faith. Deal with him on the basis of what he expresses to you about his beliefs. (You'll find he is never totally consistent with the doctrine he holds.)

E. Do not use a King James Bible. According to the teachings of some Muslim sects, King James himself translated this version and corrupted it. The New International Version is an excellent choice.

F. Never use a Bible in which you have made any marks. To a Muslim this can mean disrespect for the Word of God.

G. Avoid all pictures depicting God, Jesus or any biblical characters. To Muslims, this is idolatry.

H. Don't be offended by the Muslim's use of the term Allah. It's simply the Arabic word for God.

I. Never use the word *Trinity*. To Muslims, this word often connotes the worship of three gods and will bog you down with issues of polytheism. There are many ways to express the trinity concept. One way, for example, is to use the term *Godhead*.

J. When dealing with African-American mainline Muslims, do not initiate issues concerning race. Many African-American Muslims tend to have a humanistic slant and see themselves beyond Blackness. Therefore, racial differences should not pose barriers.

Most of all, never forget the power of love. For against love, there is no defense, Islamic or otherwise.

## IMPORTANT QUESTIONS AND ANSWERS

MUSLIMS MAY KNOW a little or a lot about Christianity, but in either case they also will have heard many things about Christians that simply aren't true. Dr. Robert Smith, senior pastor of Calvary Baptist Church in Compton, California, has given a good deal of thought to some of the questions Muslims ask, and how to prepare biblical answers in advance.

QUESTION

Western converts to Islam often express their relief to find that Islam's teaching about God is straightforward, and devoid of the mysteries of Christianity, such as the Trinity and the deity of Christ. Islam is clear in saying God is One. So they might ask something like this:

*Why do Christians cover up their absurd teachings about God by calling them a "mystery"?*

ANSWER

I have to admit that every day I have to accept things that I don't understand in order to exist and enjoy a comfortable life. I don't understand all of the dynamics that go into what makes an airplane fly, but I am not going to wait until I find out before I fly on one, because the flying of airplanes is a reality. I don't understand all the inner workings of my computer but the reality is that the computer can do some amazing things and people like me use them every day without understanding their inner functions. As a matter of fact, it is a mystery to me how a brown cow can eat green grass and produce white milk, but I drink it.

If, after so many years of scientific research, the physical universe in which we live is still beyond our complete understanding, why should we think it strange that we cannot fully understand the invisible Creator of this universe? In fact, if we could completely understand God, then we would be equal with God. The Bible reminds us, "As the heavens are higher than the earth, so are my ways higher than your ways and my thoughts than your thoughts" (Isa. 55:8,9).

Also, in Romans we read, "How unsearchable His judgments and His paths beyond tracing out" (Rom. 11:33). No one can begin to know the mind of God. But God will teach us whatever we need to know about Him if we pray and ask Him.

QUESTION

*So if you believe in the Trinity, does that mean you believe in three Gods?*

ANSWER

Jesus Himself said that God is One: "The most important one, answered Jesus, is this: 'Hear, O Israel, the Lord our God, the Lord is one" (Mark 12:29). Jesus was quoting from the Old Testament, or Torah. Let's look at the Old Testament.

The Bible categorically states twenty-eight times that God is One. Deut. 6:4-5 says, "Hear, O Israel: The Lord our God, the Lord is One. Love the Lord your God with all your heart and with all your soul and with all your strength." Deut. 4:35 says, "To you it was shown, that you might know that the LORD Himself is God; there is none other beside Him."

In the Psalms (Zabur): Ps. 86:10 says, "For you are great and do marvelous deeds; you alone are God."

In the book of the Prophets: Isa. 44:6,8 says "This is what the Lord says I am the first and I am the last; apart from me there is no God; You are my witnesses. Is there any God besides me? No, there is no other Rock; I know not one."

In the New Testament (Injil): 1 Tim. 2:5,6a says, "For there is one God and one mediator between God and men, the man Christ Jesus, who gave Himself as a ransom for all men."

1 Cor. 8:4b: "And that there is none other God but one."

1 Tim. 1:17: "Now unto the King eternal immortal, invisible, the only wise God, be honor and glory for ever and ever. Amen!"

Why not ask God to teach you the truth about Jesus: is He truly God? Ask Him to show you the truth about salvation or how to get to heaven. That is, does one have to go through Jesus

Christ in order to get to God the Father? Ask God to show you if what Christians say about Jesus Christ is true.

I am convinced that these are mysteries that God will reveal to you if you ask Him. Once I was searching for the truth about God, and Jesus Christ. As a matter of fact, I used to go to the Mosque searching, but it was not until I prayed and asked God to make Himself real to me and show me the truth about Jesus that my life changed and has never been the same.

QUESTION

*Why do you blaspheme by calling Jesus God? How can Jesus be God?*

ANSWER

John's Gospel says, "The Word (of God) became flesh and dwelt among us" (John 1:14). God in His sovereignty chose to reveal Himself to us by His Word, who became a human being and lived among us, having become one of us. The apostle Paul sums it up best when he says, concerning Jesus, "Who, being in very nature God, did not consider equality with God something to be grasped, but made Himself nothing, taking the very nature of a servant, being made in human likeness. And being found in appearance as a man, He humbled Himself and became obedient to death—even the death of the cross! Therefore God has highly exalted Him and given Him a name which is above every name," (Phil. 2:6-11).

QUESTION

*How can Jesus be God when He did things God doesn't or won't do? For example:*

♦ *Jesus prayed to God instead of to Himself.*

♦ *Jesus got hungry and thirsty (Matt. 4:1 and John 19:28), but God never gets hungry or thirsty (Ps. 50:9-13; Acts 17:25).*

♦ *Jesus was tempted by the devil (Matt. 4:1 and Heb. 4:15), but God cannot be tempted (James 1:17).*

✦ *Jesus got tired (John 4:6; Matt. 8:24), but God doesn't get tired (Ps. 121:4; Isa. 40:28).*

✦ *Jesus learned obedience and grew up into a mature and perfect man (Heb. 5:9), but God never changes (James 1:17).*

### ANSWER

Jesus is indeed God, but for our sake when He became a man, He chose no longer to function as God. He was still God and could use His powers as God, but chose instead only to function as a man.

As a human being, Jesus was born, grew in knowledge and maturity, got hungry and thirsty, got tired and sleepy, prayed to His Father in heaven, was tempted in every way that we are (but he never sinned) and died (but God raised Him up from the dead—victorious over death). All these things prove that Jesus became a real human being. Jesus is not an apparition nor was He just pretending to be a man. As a human being, He had all of our needs and limitations, except for our sinful, fallen nature. One reason Jesus is called the "last Adam" (1 Cor. 15:45) is because he became just like Adam was before He sinned.

### QUESTION

*In Islam, we live in Ummah, in fellowship with the global community of Muslims, which gives us both identity and a sense of belonging. Other than scattered little churches on street corners, what does Christianity really have to compare to Ummah?*

### ANSWER

It is true that there are local churches of all sizes, styles and sorts. But the true Church is spiritual, invisible and universal, comprised of all those who have accepted Jesus Christ into their lives as Savior and Lord. This Church of Jesus Christ is God's anointed arena where His presence and power reside, and in the midst of this redeemed and redemptive society, the rule of the Kingdom of God is being experienced by His people:

1. The Church is the place where the Gospel and the Word of God are proclaimed.

   1 Timothy 3:15, NKJV: "But if I am delayed, I write so that you may know how you ought to conduct yourself in the house of God, which is the church of the living God, the pillar and ground of the truth." 3:16: "And without controversy great is the mystery of godliness: God was manifested in the flesh, justified in the Spirit, seen by angels, preached among the Gentiles, believed on in the world, received up in glory."

2. The Church is the place where God's forgiveness and healing are experienced, through the blood of Christ.

   "Assuredly, I say to you, whatever you bind on earth will be bound in heaven, and whatever you loose on earth will be loosed in heaven. Again I say to you that if two of you agree on earth concerning anything that they ask, it will be done for them by My Father in heaven. For where two or three are gathered together in My name, I am there in the midst of them" (Matt. 18:18-20 NKJV).

3. The Church is the physical gathering place of the spiritual Body of Christ

   "For by the grace given me I say to every one of you: Do not think of yourself more highly than you ought, but rather think of yourself with sober judgment, in accordance with the measure of faith God has given you. Just as each of us has one body with many members, and these members do not all have the same function" (Rom 12:3 -4).

4. The Church, because it is made up of believers, is indwelled by the Holy Spirit's Presence and Power.

   "But Peter, standing up with the eleven, raised his voice and said to them, 'Men of Judea and all who dwell in

Jerusalem, let this be known to you, and heed my words. For these are not drunk, as you suppose, since it is only the third hour of the day. But this is what was spoken by the prophet.'"

Peter then began to quote from Joel 2: "And it shall come to pass in the last days, says God, That I will pour out of My Spirit on all flesh; your sons and your daughters shall prophesy, your young men shall see visions, your old men shall dream dreams. And on My menservants and on My maidservants I will pour out My Spirit in those days; and they shall prophesy. I will show wonders in heaven above and signs in the earth beneath: blood and fire and vapor of smoke. The sun shall be turned into darkness, and the moon into blood, before the coming of the great and notable day of the Lord. And it shall come to pass that whoever calls on the name of the Lord shall be saved" (Acts 2:14-21 NKJV).

BILL GARVEY WRITES:

At the age of sixteen, a woman heard about a "prophet" named Muhammad. She had never read about him in the Bible. Her brother had sparked her curiosity by sharing with her several books on the subject. Intrigued, she asked those in her Bible study about Muhammad, but they had no explanation.

Not only did they not want to explain, they said that since this was a Muslim belief, it was not open to discussion. This was tragic. If they had bothered to address this issue, it might have made a significant difference in the path of her search for truth.

Her research in the encyclopedia confirmed that Muhammad was an historical character. But she could not understand why he was not mentioned in the Bible. She wondered if the biblical writers were hiding something or concealing their ignorance.

She had become fed up with how her life was going—stuck in the pattern of drinking and smoking reefers on Friday and Saturday nights and going to church on Sunday mornings. She was hungry for God and really wanted to clean up her life and stop using drugs. However, she felt she wasn't getting anything out of church. She even tried to prepare herself for the Spirit by not partying at all on Saturday. She wanted to learn from the Word of God. But when the preacher's message would get interesting, he would start "whooping." This would leave her hanging and her desire for more teaching unsatisfied.

She tried to get happy and shout, but wondered why she couldn't. Eventually, her church attendance became sporadic.

The final blow for her came when she was invited to a Christmas party for the usher board. She arrived with a male friend who wanted to have some drinks before the party, but she insisted on attending the party first. She did not want her church leaders to smell alcohol on her breath.

The pastor was at the party and there was a full bar. Soon her escort called out from the kitchen, "V_____, we are going to party tonight!" Unfortunately, this was an all-too-familiar cliché from the sinful life she wanted to forsake.

She was crushed! For her, Christianity seemed morally bankrupt. Islam became the only viable alternative. In time, her search for God led her to the mosque.

She bowed toward Mecca, and she claimed that Islam gave her the spiritual resources to straighten her life out. According to V_____, Islam has gave her the moral imperative not to drink.

She explained that in Islam she prayed five times a day. Why? "Because I wanted to continually have God on my mind during the day. The Qur'an also says that you cannot be intoxicated and pray. If you pray five times a day you cannot drink."

She was a true seeker of God, but Christianity derailed her faith—at least temporarily. There are many like her "who have not bowed down to Baal"—many who want to repent from a life of sin, who are ready for the Messiah. Won't you share the Messiah with them? In fact, V—has recently accepted Jesus as Messiah and Lord of her life.

### Chapter Five Discussion Questions

1. Review Carl Ellis's study of four types of unrighteousness. Cite examples of institutional ungodliness and institutional oppression that have occurred in your community in recent years. Do you believe such corruption may have caused some Christians to abandon their faith and to turn to other religions such as Islam? What can you and your church/Christian community do to bring about change in these situations?

2. Discuss experiences you have had talking with Muslims about Jesus Christ. What was the most challenging question you were asked? Where did you find common ground? What would you do differently the next time?

3. Discuss the difference between human efforts to please God and gain salvation through righteousness and the redemption for sin accomplished by Jesus on the cross. Are these ideas incompatible? Why or why not? What scriptures support your point of view?

# 6

## WHAT ARE OUR COMMUNITY'S LONGTERM GOALS?

A S WE'VE SEEN, from the 1700s to this day, the issue of Black vs. Christian has been at the center of a great debate among African Americans. Among followers of Jesus it is a debate that has transcended our identities as Colored, Negro, Afro-American, Black or African American. Through the years, African-American Christians have also grappled with the most appropriate strategy for success in America. Should we assimilate into mainstream life or consolidate around our cultural resources? In other words, should we opt for "integration" or "Black nationalism?" "Multiculturalism" or "Afrocentrism?" What is the relationship between Afrocentrism and "Christo-centrism?" Are they compatible, incompatible or mutually exclusive?

Afrocentrism is not new to the African-American Christian community. Have you ever wondered why so many of the early African-American churches and Christian organizations had "African" in their names? For example, the African Baptist Churches, the African Methodist Episcopal Churches (AME), AME Zion Churches, the Free African Society and the African Presbyterian Churches to name a few. It is clear that they identified with Africa. Have you wondered what was behind this identification? Let's take a look.

Like the struggle for freedom and dignity, historic theology of the African-American Church developed along two streams, *northern* and *southern*. In both cases, an overarching biblical pattern and theme (paradigm) developed for doing ministry.

Of course, like all other Bible-believing communities, the historic African-American Church preached Christ crucified and risen, and the doctrines of salvation by grace through faith. The ministry paradigm came in the way the Church applied its faith to the surrounding community.

As we've seen, in the South, the theological paradigm was the "exodus." In the pre–Civil War North, where slavery was less prevalent, the theological paradigm was the "exile." The "freedmen" saw the hand of God at work. They sensed a special calling—a calling to bring the gospel of Christ to the rest of the people of African descent living in the South, Canada, the Caribbean, Africa and beyond.

By the 1820s, this Pan-African movement was well established, and it lasted through the 1880s. Rev. Nathaniel Paul, pastor of the African Baptist Society in Albany, New York, believed that people of African descent should return to Africa to spread the gospel of Christ. Rev. James Theodore Holly and Rev. Martin Robinson Delany advocated the establishment of a strong Black Christian nation in Africa or the Caribbean. They wanted to use its economic, diplomatic and military power to rescue Africa and African peoples from the destructive aims and policies of other nations. Rev. James W. C. Pennington argued that African Americans had a special obligation to become involved in African missions. Others like Rev. A. W. Hanson, Augustus Washington, and Lewis Woodson argued that the destiny of African Americans was tied up with the destiny of Africa. Rev. Alexander Crummell (mentor to W. E. B. DuBios) emphasized the need for economic development in Africa for the sake of Africans.

Had it fully developed, the North's exile-based theology would have empowered our people toward missions, while addressing the need for identity, purpose and a sense of security and significance in the economy of God. However, the end of the post–Civil War Reconstruction in the South altered this situation. The social progress of former slaves was impeded as they coped with a rising tide of terrorism and intimidation. The mission activity in Africa was devastated as colonialism consolidated its hold.

This trauma forced the Church to abandon its concern for identity and missions, and it reverted to the old survival approach. Ultimately, the Church no longer played a large role in bringing definition to the African-American experience.

With the development of urbanization came new social and cultural challenges. If the Church had addressed the issues of identity and significance in the economy of God, it would have continued to be a major player. Instead the Christian consensus began to erode. The current state of crisis in the African-American community is testimony to this. Christianity will continue to be perceived as irrelevant as long as the Church remains relatively silent regarding a theology of empowerment.

The silence of the Church will continue to facilitate the growing Islamic infiltration among African Americans. During the 1800s, when the Church spoke to the concerns of dignity, identity and significance, Islam never developed among African Americans the way it has today. Until we once again biblically address these concerns as well as the issues of pain, rage and the quest for true manhood, we will continue to see Islam attract many of our sons.

Today, Louis Farrakhan captures the imaginations of many young African-American men. Witness the tremendous turnout at the Million Man March (October 16, 1995). It is estimated that over 60 percent of those who gathered in Washington, D.C., were Christians. Many of them were outspoken about their Christian witness. However, the response to Farrakhan's call to march reveals his considerable influence. There is no Christian leader of any stripe who could have convened a million Christian and non-Christian men to take a stand for righteousness.

While it can be argued that Farrakhan employs theological smoke and mirrors in his lengthy diatribes, it cannot be denied that he touches on core cultural issues of great concern to many African Americans, especially young men. Yet the Bible deals with all these important issues better than any other book. In fact, this is why Mr. Farrakhan quotes from it so much.

The road from Christianity to the Nation of Islam to Orthodox Islam is a well-traveled one. Hundreds of thousands of young men are searching and full of questions, yet only the Word of God can really supply the answers. We can make a breakthrough for Christ among those who seek by understanding the psychology behind their drift toward Islam. Engaging them in conversation and hearing their stories is key to this understanding.

Before meaningful conversations can take place, however, walls of distrust and suspicion must come down. These walls will crumble as we communicate our desire to understand the concerns and beliefs of our young African-American men. Through understanding, wisdom and patience, we must find a way to introduce God's grace and truth to them. As we demonstrate our Christian faith in word and deed, we will begin to transform our communities, bless our families and save our sons.

## Chapter Six Discussion Questions:

1. Should African American's assimilate into mainstream life? Or should we consolidate around our cultural resources? In other words, should we opt for integration or Black Nationalism? Multiculturalism or Afrocentrism?

2. What is the relationship between Afrocentrism and Christocentrism? Are they compatible, incompatible or mutually exclusive?

3. To what do you attribute the success of Louis Farrakhan's Million Man March? Discuss why so many Christian men participated. What was their hope? Why did Farrakhan and the Nation of Islam appeal to them?

4. What are the primary issues that raised the walls of mistrust and suspicion between African Americans and Christianity? How can they be broken down?

5. Discuss and list longterm goals your church or Christian community can establish to reclaim African-American youth for the Gospel.

శ్రీ

# MY SPIRITUAL BATTLE

*By Jason Culpepper*

A S IN THE case of many African Americans who call themselves Muslims, I would describe my involvement with the Nation of Islam as "in again—out again." I never fully submitted to the Muslim faith because I was a seeker.

I was born in Atlanta, Georgia, on December 17, 1947. When I was eight years old, a preacher named Elder Welch came and held tent meetings in town. There were healings and other powerful demonstrations of God's grace. My grandmother (a member of the Church of Christ) and aunt (a Charismatic) took me to the first meeting. My grandmother got angry over doctrine and had nothing to do with the rest of the revival. But my aunt took me to the rest of the meetings. I don't remember outwardly responding to the gospel invitation, yet I was deeply impressed with Elder Welch. I saw the power of God in him. To me, this was a way to be in God's grace. I decided to become a part of his ministry when I grew up.

*Voices*

I was on fire for God and only wanted to live for Him and serve Him. I even used to practice preaching. Apparently, the enemy heard this.

When I was about ten, my parents could no longer take care of my brother, sister and me, so they sent us to Temple, Georgia, to live with our grandparents. I feared my grandmother. She often got angry and whipped me severely. My grandfather owned timberland with several houses on it. In one of these houses lived a pipe-smoking old lady from Louisiana who was into some pretty weird stuff. Sometimes I ran from my grandmother's beatings and hid in her house.

The first time I went there she said to me, "I can give you something that will stop the pain." I looked at her and she started laughing. I tried to ignore her for a while, but she cooked little teacakes that I loved to eat. One day when I was alone with her, she said again, "Jason, I can give you something that will stop the pain." I really didn't want to get into anything weird, but the pain of my grandmother's beatings was more than I could bear. So one night I went to her house for her remedy. The first thing she did was to swear me to secrecy. Then she had me recite some chants, inhale some strange smelling stuff and drink some bitter liquid. As soon as I drank this liquid, I passed out. When I regained consciousness, I knew something had changed. Something was in me and with me. She gave me a little bag of horrible smelling herbs and told me, "As long as you carry this bag, nothing will harm you." From that day, I found myself wanting to hurt something or somebody. The next whipping I got from my grandmother didn't hurt. Though she used a hickory stick, I looked at her and started smiling. Before, I was a smart kid in school. Now I couldn't learn. I got into fights and dabbled in the occult. I became wild and extremely self-centered. Every now and then I would hear voices, and some had foreign accents.

### "Your Brother"

My grandmother's beatings, which were directed at me and left scars, could not get me to behave. When I was twelve, my grandmother was arrested for child abuse. My whole family was angry with me for being a witness against her. As a result, I was sent back to Atlanta to live with my mother. By that time my parents had broken up.

In Atlanta, I started setting fires, torturing animals, and doing things out of pure meanness. I couldn't wait to grow up so I could torture humans the way I was torturing animals. I was driven toward violence and I had no control over it. It's a miracle that I didn't hurt or kill anybody during those years.

My father lost his eyesight as the result of an accident in Clearwater, Florida. I had come to hate him because he abandoned me when I needed him the most. Now, he needed me to take care of him. We had some serious conflicts. As I got older, I began to look for the "baddest dude in town" to be with. Good people turned me off. I began to challenge death through drag racing. In fact, I learned to drive by stealing cars and trucks.

When I was about thirteen, I heard that the Louisiana lady had died and it had a profound effect on me. I grieved tremendously and the evil influences on me increased. As I got into more trouble with the police, they took me to psychiatrists to find out what was wrong with me.

One day I saw a huge diamondback rattlesnake at the zoo. He rattled at me and a voice said, "This is your brother." Suddenly, I had a strong desire to reach in and touch the snake. I was in a trance until my friend pulled me away.

Eventually, I was sent to the reformatory at Marianna, Florida. It resembled a college campus with no fences or walls. Yet they made it very clear that if you tried to escape, you would be taken to the "White House"—the place where they beat those who misbehaved. In the White House was a room with a chin-high bar they would make you hold on to while you got your lashes. If you were due to get one hundred lashes and let the bar go at ninety-nine, you would get one hundred more.

I tried to escape but was quickly recaptured and taken to the White House. The guards couldn't figure out how I could take so many lashes and not be bothered. One of them told me, "Don't you ever think about running again! If you do, you'll get double the punishment you just got!"

Within minutes, I took off again. They chased me but I got away. I hid in a boxcar for three days hoping the train would pull out, but it never did. Eventually, hunger drove me to return to the reformatory. I got double punishment, but it didn't faze me. I ended up staying there a little over a year. The usual time spent there was about six months.

When I got out I didn't go home. I went to Perry, Florida—a place where Blacks were not allowed uptown after dark. I went to work for a man named Red Patch, who owned a large logging company. I wanted to straighten out my life and become a heavy equipment operator. Red Patch had me digging up stumps instead. One day on the job, I felt a sting on my leg like a bumblebee. It was the bite of a rattler. One of my coworkers knocked me out of the way and cut the snake in half. I was rushed to the emergency room where the doctor told me how fortunate I was that the snake didn't do more harm. I thought, "That's because the snake was my brother."

Later I confronted Mr. Patch and said, "I can't do this kind of work any more. You promised to teach me heavy equipment operation."

He replied, "I don't think that type of work is what a nigger needs. A nigger has to use his back."

When I refused to go back to work, Mr. Patch picked up a tree limb and said, "Come here boy."

"I dare you to make me come over there!" I snarled at him.

Suddenly I realized that it wasn't me speaking. It was a demon. This response scared Mr. Patch so much that he dropped the limb, backed up, and went for his gun. One of my coworkers urged me to flee, and I did—through the woods.

My hatred for this man was so strong that I stole a rifle and hid in the trees in front of his house. As he came out I opened fire on him, emptying the magazine. Miraculously, he wasn't hit. I was being driven into self-destructive behavior.

*"Violent Thing"*

Some time later, I found myself in a boring church service. An old lady told me, "God has a calling on your life." My first impulse was to growl at her.

Three days later I was hit by a car. My pelvis was broken into twenty-seven pieces, my ribs were broken, I had a concussion, and one leg and both knees were broken. I shouldn't have survived. While in a coma, I had a vision of myself standing in a circle of angels who were trying to protect me from surrounding demons. But I was trying to get out of the circle to contact the demons. I didn't understand what all this meant then. But the experience heightened my interest on the occult.

When I was released from the hospital I tried to straighten my life out again. Instead, I started stealing cars and ended up in jail. This time I met some Muslim brothers. They told me that Islam was what I needed. Unlike the brothers on the street, they were studying Arabic. At meetings we discussed how we were going to kill the White man. They called me "Killer" because I loved to fight and was always mean.

Once I got out of jail, I went to St. Petersburg, Florida, where I got involved in the Jo Mo Gang, which were connected with the Black Panther Party. As time passed, several gang members disappeared and others were shot to death. We suspected the CIA was involved.

Soon, a brother from the Nation of Islam began to tell us, "This violent thing is going to get you killed. Come into the Nation, and you will be protected." This rekindled my interest in the Nation. As I studied their teachings, I thought I was getting control of this evil force that was driving me to my death.

One night I was singing at an amateur night show. One of the other performers started kidding me, pretending to ridicule me. The organizer of the show didn't realize it was a joke. He intervened and said, "That ain't no way to treat this man." Then he said to me, "You'll forgive him won't you."

The performer said, "I was just playing. Besides, Jesus can forgive anybody."

The name Jesus infuriated me!

He said, "I'm sorry. I'm a Christian."

At the word *Christian* I lost control and attacked him. Before I realized it, I had my hands around his neck. My only thought was to rip his head off. I wanted to kill him!

How dangerous was that demonic force inside me!

I decided to leave Florida and go to Memphis, Tennessee. By this time, I considered myself a Muslim. In reality, I was a strong sympathizer. I ended up working with Isaac Hayes and Stax Records. One evening at a company party, I was obsessed with the thought of taking a gun and killing everybody there. The only thing that stopped me was a girl who liked me. She dragged me away from the party and took me to her house.

Finally, I started meeting with the Muslim brothers again. They would say to me, "What you need is the knowledge we can give you. You can be a strong warrior for the Nation. You can be in the jihad against the White man." So I resumed my studies under the Nation of Islam.

*Laughter*

One evening, I was on my way to do a show for Stax Records, dressed up for the occasion. When I stopped at a convenience store, some thugs beat me up, robbed me and stole my car. I was once again hospitalized with several broken ribs. After my discharge, I ended up working as assistant manager for a chain of restaurants called Lobe's Bar-B-Q.

The restaurant where I worked closed for a week for spring cleaning and Jimmy, the manager, hired some temporary help. Two of these guys were the ones who mugged me at the convenience store and stole my car. They had the nerve to brag about what they did to me. Because I was quiet, they thought I was a pushover.

I got Jimmy's loaded .38 from his office. My intention was to kill them both—shooting them in the leg, then the hip, then the side, and finally in the head. When Jimmy discovered his gun missing, he came out of his office and warned the guys that I was armed. I went crazy and started shooting until no bullets were left. I hit one of the guys as he ran out the front door. The other one ducked behind the counter. I put the gun to his head. He begged me not to shoot him.

I heard a voice say, "He's dead."

I pulled the trigger, heard a bang and saw his brains splatter all over the place. At least that's what I thought I heard and saw. But there were no bullets.

I threw down the gun and fled through the back door. I was halfway across Memphis when I realized I had left everything back at the restaurant. When I returned there were police everywhere. I was quickly identified and arrested. When they put me in the car, I saw the guy I thought I had killed. I was shocked. Just then I heard a voice laughing. I knew I had deep problems.

I was sentenced to six months at a penal farm. Again I began to study with the Islamic brothers. I also prayed, "Allah, I need help. Whoever you are, I need help!" I was afraid that I was going to kill somebody or get killed. But I got no reply from Allah. To make matters worse, I ran into the brother of the man I shot at Lobe's Bar-B-Q and his two cousins. The brother told me, "I just want you to know, you belong to us."

The anger in me began to rear its ugly head again. I got a thick industrial-sized mop handle, broke it in half and hid it in my pants leg. I waited for the right time and hit a home run on the back of that brother's head. I was driven by a voice saying, "More!"

Every time he screamed, "Lord, please don't kill me!" I said, "Yeah, you're dead homie!" By the time a guard stopped me that brother was messed up. I again heard that demonic laughter.

One night I had a vivid dream that I was going to hell, but I had grown so cold and calloused that I didn't care. I couldn't cry. Nothing could break me.

## Tripped

I returned to Tallahassee, Florida, and got a job as an auto mechanic. There, I met a young man who was on fire for God. He told me God had sent him to me and I hated him for it. It unnerved me just to be around him, especially when he would tell me that Jesus loved me. There was something about him that frightened me. I was afraid to touch him because I knew he was a child of God.

Eventually, this man got married and left town. The night he left, he came to the repair shop just to see me. He told me emphatically, "God has a call on your life. You belong to Him. This calling is from years back, beyond your awareness or control. One day you are going to be backed into a corner, ready to hurt or kill somebody. On that day, before you do anything drastic, call on the name of Jesus."

Instead of considering Jesus, however, I got more involved with Islam. I returned to Atlanta to live. There, I started stockpiling guns for the coming Black/White war the Nation of Islam was telling me about. I also started stealing cars again.

One night, I was almost caught with a stolen car when the police rounded up several members of our theft ring. When I learned that my name was on the police computer, I fled to Carrollton, Georgia. There, I started selling dope on the side. The corrupt sheriff in Carroll County busted me for drug dealing, but instead of arresting me, he demanded that I sell drugs for him. I was afraid of his Mafia connections, so I promptly quit selling drugs and got a job at a garage.

The owner of the garage and I clashed because he confiscated my tools and refused to pay me. I was so angry I decided to get revenge. One night I broke into his garage, loaded every tool I could find onto his beautiful classic '65 Ford pickup truck and prepared to drive off. I must have made a lot of noise because the people in a hotel across the street called the police.

At the sound of the sirens, I tried to start the truck but it wouldn't crank. The engine was missing. I fled on foot, running past a cop. Just as he shot at me I tripped over something and fell. I never saw what I tripped on. If I hadn't tripped, the bullet would have struck me in the middle of the back. Before I could get up the police surrounded and arrested me.

*Delivered*

Back in jail, I got deeper into the teachings of the Nation of Islam. In my mind, Allah was still the way. This was reinforced by some negative memories of so-called Christians. For example, when I was younger, I saw a TV minister preaching against Blacks being in America. When I was just a kid, the KKK burned my grandmother's house down and killed my infant uncle. To me this was Christianity.

My cellmate was a three-hundred-pound man named Perry Holms. For some strange reason, he liked the top bunk. From day one we didn't get along. I threw coffee into the face of a guard and was severely beaten for it. During that time, demonic voices returned, harassing me and driving me to say vicious things. After the beating, a Muslim brother across the cellblock told me, "Brother, I'm praying to Allah that you get some peace." My cellmate told me, "Why don't you shut your mouth." I told him to mind his own business. At that, he jumped down from his bunk to attack me, but I used his momentum to ram his head into the bars. He was out cold with a concussion. The guards quickly subdued me. All I remember is being pinned against the wall.

I came to with a pounding headache. I was confined in a padded cell and had a straitjacket on. Demonic voices flooded my mind. Finally, a guard came to check on me. He asked, "Are you all right now? Look at your head." He told me that after they pinned me against the wall, I broke free and rammed my own head into the bars. I knew I was about die or go crazy. Suddenly, through all these voices, I remembered the young man from Tallahassee, Florida saying, "Call on the name of Jesus."

Instead, I called out to Allah, "I want to die." Every time I repeated this prayer, the more miserable I was—the more I heard the demonic voices laughing.

Finally, I called out, "Jesus, I want to die. Can you please kill me?" Just then I heard a demonic voice saying, "Don't pray to Jesus, pray to me. I'm Allah!" I heard other demonic voices screaming. My head felt like it was going to blow up. All of a sudden, something happened. For the first time in almost twenty years I began to cry. The more I cried, the more I wanted to cry. I sobbed, "God am I really dying? Please kill me!"

Finally God spoke to me, "I won't kill what's not mine."

I pleaded to God, "Then take me, I'm yours."

The demonic voices left immediately. As I continued to cry, I began to realize that it wasn't Allah who delivered me. It was Jesus!

When the guards came to check on me, I said to them, "I need a Bible, quick!" Because I was in a straitjacket, I had to use an unsharpened pencil to turn the pages. I devoured the Bible, even in the dark. (For that reason I wear glasses today.) The fact that I was going to court the next week as a three-time loser didn't matter to me any more. All that mattered was Jesus Christ, who saved my life. In time, one of the guards said to me, "You've changed my life. I know what you were, and I don't see that anymore. You were on your way to die, but you have totally changed."

At my trial, I expected to get twenty-five years to life. But due to some unusual circumstances, I ended up with an eight-year sentence. From that time in prison to this day, I've been on fire for God.

I have since shared my testimony with many Muslim brothers. I often tell them, "I know the voice I heard claiming to be Allah was not. I realize that Allah is the Arabic word for God."

I also challenge them by asking, "Why would the demons try to get me to call on the name of Allah if there was saving power in him?

"And why did they try to stop me from calling on the name of Jesus if there was no saving power in His name?"

# SAVING MY SON

### By Wilford Darden

THIS STORY STARTS somewhere in 1976. I was in a group of young men drinking beer, smoking marijuana, and discussing the future. The future did not include getting a higher education. For the most part it included getting a good job while continuing to do drugs, drink and party. The reason for the group meeting was because I had just received an incomplete in my college air conditioning course, and I did not know how to explain it to my father who really wanted me to have a marketable skill. My father's philosophy was if a man has a skill he will never have to be out of work. I did not want to face him, especially in light of the fact that my younger brother had received a four-year track-and-field scholarship to Grambling State University.

## THE VISION

THE CONVERSATION CONTINUED and soon it was my turn to discuss my idea of the future. I thought my vision was clear and plain. I told the group I wanted to get a good job, get married and buy a home, a car and a truck. I wanted to have two sons who would continue to preserve my family heritage.

Well, in an amazing chronicle of events, that vision started to unfold just as I had imagined it. In January of 1977 I got a good job at the city's largest utility company. In June of the same year I got married to Nita. In March of 1978 I bought a new Z-28 Camaro and one of my uncles sold me a 1963 Ford truck, which I restored to new. In August of 1979 our first son was born, and that December we closed escrow on a new home. You'd think I would have thanked God for His blessings on my life, but I didn't. Even as my drinking and drug use increased, in August of 1985 our second son was born, thus completing the vision.

Or so I thought.

## SON SWAPPING

OUR SECOND SON was a joy to all of our lives, but our first son was not.

We were in awe of our lives and the way everything was unfolding. Our friends and family loved our second son. Meanwhile, our first son fought for his first place, and for attention. The good life that I was experiencing was not expressed in thanksgiving to the Lord. Although Nita was brought up in a godly home, and continually tried to get me to attend church with her and the boys, the drug culture had a serious hold on me. I could not find the strength needed to change. In fact there were many Sunday mornings when, on her way to church, Nita would have to step over me lying on the floor, sick from the night before. I would always ask her pray for me and she would say, "I have to" as she closed the door.

I would discover later in life that my oldest son remembered these events all too well. They presented challenges for all of us that went beyond what we had imagined.

**POINT:** *When it comes to saving our sons, one of the greatest tools in the hands of God is genuine love for Him, expressed in our daily situations and circumstances in front of our children. Unfortunately, divorce and the focus*

*of materialism are invading many African-American homes and commu-*
*nities. Who is going to pay the price?*

*If I could have a word with young Christian parents concerning*
*early childhood development (a very special component to saving our*
*sons), I would say this: focus on the biblical values you want your child*
*to demonstrate and teach them through example—in the midst of life sit-*
*uations and circumstances.*

*"You shall love the Lord with all your heart, with all your soul, and with*
*all your strength. And these words which I command you today shall be in*
*your heart. You shall teach them diligently to your children, and shall talk*
*of them when you sit in your house, when you walk by the way, when you*
*lie down, and when you rise up" (Deuteronomy 6:5-7).*

I believe my lack of thanksgiving to God led to the tragic events
that followed. In January 1985, death invaded our lives and took the
life of our second son. He died from what is called Sudden Infant
Death Syndrome—SIDS—in his sleep at the babysitter's home.
This tragedy shattered me because my dream life was crumbling
before my eyes. It shattered by wife because she felt as if she should
have been at home caring for her baby instead of working. But it
caused temporal joy to our first son because he returned to the center of attention for a season.

Yet, God was at work on another plan. At the funeral, the pastor that
preached the sermon said to me, "Keep your hands in His hands."

I loved that son so much I did not ever want to forget him. So I
began to ask every person that I thought was a Christian, "How can
I know beyond a shadow of a doubt that Heaven is real and that people actually go there?"

Surprisingly, the answer I received was, "You must have faith."

I was from the streets, and the concept of faith was foreign to my
understanding. My response was, "Just tell me yes or no!"

I could not find anyone that would say a definite yes. They continued to give me answers about faith instead.

## THE SEARCH FOR TRUTH

SINCE THE ANSWERS were not to my satisfaction, I began to ask other groups the same questions. For example, the Jehovah's Witnesses told me about a place called Paradise Earth.

The Nation of Islam talked about the resurrection of the mind. They explained that Heaven is a lie of the White man to get Blacks focused on the pie in the sky that would never materialize while the Black man catches Hell on earth.

One day on my way to work I was channel surfing. On KHCB (105.7) I heard someone say that you could be sure that Heaven is real by accepting Jesus as your Lord. He went on to say, "Repeat these words after me . . . "

I pulled the car over and repeated the words. What I now realize is the Lord took His blessings in my life to another level simply by swapping sons. He took my son to be with Him, and gave me His Son to live in my heart. That's a pretty good deal!

## A FAMILY GOING SEPARATE WAYS

My new relationship with the God of the universe was bittersweet. It was bitter because my focus on the Lord consumed all of my time. Instead of focusing on the one son I had left, and contributing to his emotional stability, I would go to Bible study and church whenever the doors were open—not to mention reading as much material as I could concerning the things of the Lord.

My family was very concerned about me, so much so that they thought I had lost my mind. I stopped doing drugs and drinking; I replaced them with witnessing after work, and starting phone Bible studies. All this was sweet because for the first time in years I was sober and began to see more money in our home. In fact, the family took a trip to Disney World in Florida with the funds I saved by not taking drugs.

My oldest son was six years of age when his brother passed. The guilt of competing for attention began to haunt him and depression set in. While I was busy running after the Lord, I forgot my fatherly responsibility to my surviving boy. My wife was afraid of me; she thought I was a religious fanatic, so she began to try to get me to drink just one beer a day. I was attending church so often she thought I was having an affair with someone at the church. This caused her to follow me each time I attended. Small arguments began to take place. Even now they remind me of Jesus' words in Mathew 10: 34-36 (NIV):

> Do not think that I came to bring peace on earth. I did not come to bring peace but a sword. For I have come to set a man against his father, a daughter against her mother, and a daughter-in-law against her mother-in-law; and a man's enemies will be those of his own household.

Six months after my youngest son's death, our entire family's view of the world was headed in separate directions. Mine was a search for my identity in Christ, my wife's was in the religious traditions of the Church, and my son was in search of something or someone who could stop his deep inner pain. This inner pain was now consuming his thoughts, feelings and worst of all his character and personality. There I was standing at a crossroad experiencing the joy of the Lord, yet watching what looked like devastation of my family life. The joy of the Lord was truly my strength.

## THE WAY, THE TRUTH AND THE LIFE

FOURS YEARS LATER, I had moved up in my church (Brentwood Baptist) from adult Sunday school teacher to deacon and finally to youth director. I had also started listening to a new preacher on the radio by the name of Tony Evans and had attended his first conference on biblical exposition and discipleship. I had also been listening to Walter Martin of the Christian Research Institute, who introduced me to the science of apologetics. Now the confused pieces of the puzzle were starting to make sense. Being a youth director was a plus, because I began to see the loneliness in the heart of my son. The discipleship courses confirmed my conviction about working with others, but not my own family.

So I started a family ministry in my home, which allowed me to focus on my family. The family ministry concept allowed our family to minister to all of our friends. Our goal was for our family to glorify God. My wife and I already had one son in heaven with the Lord, so we got busy working on the other one.

He would bring his friends over for Bible study and they would clean the garage. I would pay them, then they would buy food and we would feed the panhandlers and the homeless, and then share Christ with them. Over the next year we discovered that Jesus's reality of truth was beginning to heal our wounds. We truly found a better life than the one we'd had before the tragedy. My son and his friends were at our home at least four nights a week, my wife started a senior citizens ministry for the elderly and I began to minister to Jehovah's Witnesses, those in the Nation of Islam and members of the United Pentecostal church. I also developed a ministry that helped Christians to be more confident in witnessing.

I taught everybody I could what I had learned in my search for Heaven.

## FIGHTING THE GOOD FIGHT

Things were going so well that in July of 1990 we started a non-profit organization and named it Jesus Is Alpha and Omega Ministry. This ministry focused on giving an apologetic response to those lost in cults, the occult and false religions. Our primary target area was the African-American minority community. Our main goal was to develop an army of apologists. I was convinced that once African Americans could give biblical answers for their faith, we would witness genuine revival in our communities. For the next three years we structured the organization, developed materials, and I began to move away from the family life that was working so well for us. Instead, I pursued a different love—the love of God's call on my life.

I could not believe how easy it was to witness to Muslims in the Nation of Islam. Even though I had not been able to set up a Bible study with them I was sure that it was only a matter of time before I did.

Then something happened that would rock my world to a point of almost no return. It was a warm evening in April of 1994 when the Nation of Islam minister Louis Farrakhan was scheduled to arrive, having been invited to speak at Pleasant Grove Baptist Church. I could not believe that a Baptist pastor would do such a thing as invite him to his church. Our normal procedure for doing battle with the Nation was threefold. First, we would have a person with a tape recorder interviewing the attendees of the meeting and the interviewer would share Christ with those being interviewed. On all of the vehicles we would place printed material contrasting Christian doctrine to that of the nature of the Nation of Islam. And finally, we would wait until Farrakhan stood up to speak, then our apologist would share Christ with the members of the Fruit of Islam (Farrakhan's security system) who stood around the entire facility. We have found this witnessing strategy most effective when dealing with those involved in cultic thought such as the Nation.

To make a long story short, I spoke out firmly and boldly about this situation, which I considered a blasphemy. I ended up quitting my job. Not long thereafter, my wife lost her job, too.

## BATTLE WOUNDS OF THE FAITH

MEANWHILE, MY SON moved into serious rebellion, causing havoc in all of his classes at school. It was so serious that we had him committed to a teen halfway house. After he was released he ran away from home, and we did not know where to find him. I did not discover until later that he was angry with me because I left my job, and because of this anger would not obey any instruction I gave him. We fought all the time, and my father was the only one who could bring any peace.

My son loved my father and did not mind living in his home, but my father had his problems, too. A year later my father died, and my son was devastated. The first time we noticed that he was experimenting with drugs was after my father's funeral. Then things really got bad. My son would verbally attack me publicly with the intent to harm me if he could. I was now in a true battle of saving my son.

The wisdom of the Lord reminded me that the Word of God brings life and not death. Our entire neighborhood was watching, as they were aware that our home was a godly home. Many of my son's friends that did not have fathers in their homes would stop by for fatherly advice from me. My wife was working with older women who had husbands involved in drugs and alcohol, sharing biblical ways to minister to their husbands thus removing their feeling of helplessness.

But at the same time, my son moved from using drugs to selling drugs from our home. It was so bad that we could not leave money or our car keys lying around for fear that he would take them.

Meanwhile Farrakhan planned to march on Washington and many African-American pastors had decided to go with him. Our radio broadcast was a live call-in show and we began to blast the pastors we knew that were going to the March. Again I wondered if I had truly counted the cost. Many of my friends were angry because they viewed our method of exposing the pastors as attacking God's anointed. They thought it was betrayal because we were separating ourselves from the unity of our culture.

At this point I was beginning to spiral downward in my faith. By now our entire ministry funds were gone. We had to abandon our radio broadcast owing $2,400. I had taken a position in a church as youth director but controversy followed me there as well. I established a youth discipleship movement, but an associate pastor at the church went to the senior pastor and demand that I be removed. The parents got together to fight for my tenure but the scene was brutal. I had been making $400 a month and now that was gone. It was really bad! My son's worst fears for the future of our family had come true.

**POINT:** *It is very important to understand that God has to mature us as fathers by filling us with His Word before we are going to be effective in saving our sons.*

## TWENTY-FIRST CENTURY PRODIGAL SON

BY THIS TIME, my son has gone from very bad to worse. His drug use led him from the gateway drug of marijuana to a new drug called "wet." This drug gave him tremendous confidence and strength. While under its influence he decided he was going to put me out of my home so he could take care of his mother. On one occasion he decided to take our car without asking, so I called the police and reported the car stolen. The police stopped him and the officer (who was African American) called our home and asked me what I wanted to do with him.

Was I going to lose my son? I prayed for wisdom and then I thought of David and Absalom, also Eli and his two boys and what happened when the father did not personally discipline them. I told the officer to jail him. The officer, with a voice of concern, asked me if I was sure, and with an unsure voice I said yes. Our son remained in police custody for six months. This was the first of a series of times that I would send him to jail.

Meanwhile our witnessing team had to come to grips with something the "brothers" in the Nation of Islam kept asking, "What alternative will we have if we leave the Nation and become Christians? Sing in the choir? Usher? Become a deacon?" When you start helping the "brothers" in jail or on the streets, it's important to provide a viable alternative for them. Thus our men-at-risk program was born, which we called the Integrity Plus Lawn Maintenance Program of Houston. A pastor friend of mine and I also started a "house of refuge" (staying away from the term halfway house) called Project Sunrise. Project Sunrise was a place for biblical instruction and Integrity Plus was the work program that discipled the men on the job. These two programs would serve our cause in two ways at once. It would work with African-American males in bondage to bad habits, completing their time in prison and drug addictions, but it would also serve as a witnessing tool to the brothers in the Nation of Islam.

What I was not aware of was that God was actually doing all this for me to save my son.

> **POINT:** *If we are going to be effective in saving our sons we must maintain a constant awareness of the fact that even if our priorities change concerning our sons, God remains faithful.*

## THE SHOWDOWN

I had to deal with some serious characters in the lawn maintenance program. Most of the men in the program had the same mindset as my son. So, as I worked with them, God was actually preparing me to minister to my son. And I was going to need all the training provided. One day when I arrived home my son was attempting to take the keys of our car from my wife. His eyes were bucked and he was very sweaty. My son and wife both had their hands on the strap of her purse. She said to him, "Give me my purse" and he said, "Give me the keys."

As I attempted to intercede he threw me on the floor. He then moved toward his mother's purse to get the keys. Fortunately, she managed to move the purse before he could get them. I screamed for her to call the police so we could again have him locked down.

While she called the police my son began to throw rocks through the windows of our home. By the time they arrived every window in our home was broken and all of the tires on the lawn equipment were flat. The windows in the two trucks were broken. My son was gone. To make matters worse, it began to rain. This episode started at about 9 P.M. and finally ended around 4 A.M. My wife and I had to spend the night in a Motel Six. Early the next morning I called the police to meet me at my home.

My son's friends could not believe that drugs could have such a destructive effect on him. Many of them were angry with my son because I was the only father figure they knew. Even though the previous night was horrible, I loved my son and I knew that I had to save him. As his father I believed I had a lifelong responsibility to get him back to the loving grace of the Master, which would save him from eternal doom. As his father I have to save him from himself, too, and from the satanic system that would view him as just another number in a prison cell. I had to try to save him from a society that will remember all the wrong he's done and not focus on all the potential he has.

In fact, that's what the Lord Jesus does for all of us.

Well, as we focused on repairing tires, replacing the windows in our home and on the vehicles, my son must have taken another dose. We saw him walking down the middle of the street calling my name and chanting to everyone that he was going to beat me up and take my home away. He saw me and ran toward me tearing his shirt off. I noticed a pipe close by and grabbed it for safety. Meanwhile a female police officer who was pulling up and thought that I was the aggressor. She grabbed me and handcuffed me.

My son ignored the officer's call to stop and flipped her on the ground. By the grace of God he was not shot. Instead, the officer called for backup. They finally subdued him and took him to jail. This time he went to state prison for eighteen months. We placed him on every prayer list we knew of, because we were no longer fighting flesh and blood, but spiritual wickedness in high places (Eph. 6:11-13).

# LET'S KILL THE FATTED CALF

OUR SON'S YEAR and a half of jail time was a relief to my wife and me for many reasons. We could finally sleep without concern for our son's nightly activities—sneaking in while we were asleep, taking money or keys to the car or truck. I had long slept with one eye open just to make sure that he did not come in and try to assault me. Sometimes the sound of broken glass still causes my wife to reflect back to that terrible night. Our spiritual, mental and emotional wounds were in critical condition and in need of proper healing. The state prison term was the longest time my son ever spent behind bars. We knew that he was standing at the crossroad of life with some great decisions to make. We all needed that time to think things through.

> **POINT:** *When a son has taken his parents through literal Hell is he worth saving? Is it true when the Bible says love will cover a multitude of sin? Is our own flesh and blood worth killing a fatted calf for after he has made a complete fool of himself? Think. Does the forgiveness that is discussed in the Scriptures really have the power to reconcile and restore? You bet it does!*

We visited our son in prison as often as we could. Our family goal was to see the entire family involved in ministry in some fashion and we were determined by God's grace to see it happen. Our Christian friends prayed for him and mailed him letters. It was good to know that the Body of Christ was working with us in an attempt to save our son. One night as I talked to the Lord about my boy, and the story of the lost son in Luke 15:11-32 came to mind. I asked Him, "What would the fatted calf look like today?"

The story of the lost son found in Luke's gospel is one where the son doesn't have enough respect for his family's goals to work alongside them. The father's attitude is especially interesting to me because He is the key to the eternal benefit of the son. Many times we fathers are guilty of only looking at the temporal values in our offspring, and not their eternal value.

The wise father in Luke's Gospel used the fatted calf as a bonding tool, allowing it to reintroduce eternal truths into the son's belief system. Once the eternal truths are reinserted the process of saving the son has begun. This process holds true for us as well. Like most families, when our sons were young we taught them our perspective of family values. Then they went into the world only to have those values tested. We all need a "fatted calf" as a bonding agent to return our family values to them after they come to themselves and return home.

On the day he was released from prison we drove our son to his own small apartment. He had a job waiting for him, working with me in the Integrity Plus Lawn Maintenance Program. Friends of ours gave him some furniture; my mother gave him a new television. For now he is driving one of the trucks that he had damaged in the disturbance at my home until he earns enough money to buy his own vehicle. He has a lot of things to work on before he actually reaches his potential, but that's alright!

That's why I am here: to save my son. And I shall be here until death do us part!

# OTHER ISLAMIC GROUPS

## THE HANAFIS

IN 1950, KHALIFA Hamaas Abdul Khaalis (Ernest T. McGee) joined the Nation of Islam in an attempt to bring the sect into line with Orthodox Sunni Islam. By 1956, he had become national secretary. However, his efforts proved unsuccessful. He claims that he taught Malcolm X about Orthodox Islam when Malcolm visited him at his home. In 1958, Khalifa Hamaas Abdul Khaalis broke with Elijah Muhammad and founded the Al-Hanif, Hanafi, Madh-Hob Center, Islam Faith, United States of America, American Mussulmans.

Fifteen mosques followed Khaalis with about 15,000 members. The best-known mosque was the Yasin Mosque—led by Abdula Rahman. Khalifa Hamaas Abdul Khaalis moved his family to a house in pricy section of Georgetown in Washington, D.C., where the sect was based. The house was purchased by Kareem Abdul Jabar. The Hanafis still adhere to the basic tenants of Sunni Islam.

The Hanafi Muslims gained notoriety in January 1973 when eight members of the Philadelphia Nation of Islam broke into Khaalis's house and brutally murdered seven Hanafis; five were members of Khaalis's immediate family.

In 1977, the Hanafis again captured national headlines when they tried to stop the screening of the movie *Mohammad, Messenger of God.* They did this by seizing three buildings in Washington, D.C.: the District Building (City Hall), the B'nai B'rith Building and the Islamic Center. They took several hostages. Several were injured and one was killed. Khalifa Hamaas Abdul Khaalis was sentenced to 21 to 120 years for his role in these seizures.

## THE FIVE PERCENTERS

Clarence 13X was a member in the Nation of Islam's Temple #7. He taught that the Black man was the God of the universe and had his origins in Mecca. His iconoclastic teachings resulted in his suspension from the Nation of Islam. In 1964, he founded the Five Percent Nation of Islam (also known as the Five Percent Nation or the Five Percenters). In 1969, Clarence 13X died of suspicious causes at the age of forty. Those who followed him referred to him as "Father Allah."

The Five Percenters agree with Elijah Muhammad's teaching that the White man is the Devil. However, they also include all unscrupulous and deceitful people in this category regardless of color. They also believe that the Black race was the original race and the creator of civilization. For the Five Percenters the demographics of the African-American community break down as follows:

85 percent—The masses who are ignorant of true 'divine self'
10 percent—The corrupt rulers over the 85 percent
5 percent—The truly righteous who are the followers of Father Allah

The Five Percenters are very influential in today's youth pop culture. Many of the most influential rap artists today are Five Percenters. Among the Rappers who propagate the doctrine of the Five

Percenters are: King Sun, the Supreme Team, Lakim Shabazz, Rakim Allah, Brand Nubian and the Poor Righteous Teachers.

Some Islamic sects sprang up without growing out of the Moorish Temple of Science. Among them are the Ahmadiyya Movement in Islam, U.S.A. and the Nubian Islamic Hebrews. The Nubians generally address themselves to the issue of African-American identity. The Ahmadiyyas generally do not.


*Darul Islam*

Darul Islam was founded around 1972 and developed into the largest indigenous African-American Sunni Muslim organization. The name of the organization comes from *Dar al-Islam* (house of Islam). Imam Yahya Abdul Karim was the *Amir al-Mu'mineen* (leader of the faithful). Several ministries and services were set up to serve the community, including defense, finance, education, external affairs, social services and mosques.

Darul Islam became a national movement with mosques in the United States and Canada. In the early 1980s, a man named Jaylani arrived in New York. He was a Pakistani Sufi sheikh and started teaching in one of the Darul mosques. News of his knowledge and rumored miracles rapidly spread throughout the Darul movement. People gathered around him and gave him their loyalty as a "holy man." Eventually many in the Darul movement asked Yahya Abdul Karim to yield to the leadership of Jaylani. As a result, the Darul community fell apart.

Those who remained loyal to Sheikh Jaylani formed a new group—the Fuqara. This group had a strict Sufi orientation. By 1990, most who remained loyal to Yahya Abdul Karim had disbanded and joined other Muslim groups.

Today, a small mosque in a low-income community in southeast Atlanta, Georgia, is all that is left of Darul Islam. It is led by Imam Jamil Abdullah Al-Amin—better known as H. "Rap" Brown, the former leader of the Student Nonviolent Coordinating Committee (SNCC).

During his SNCC days, he popularized the phrase, "Burn baby burn." However, unlike his past reputation, he is very mild mannered.


### The Calistron

In 1970, towards the closing years of Elijah Muhammad's leadership, a splinter group called the Calistron broke with the Nation of Islam. They saw the need to be more nationalistic and militant than the parent group. It had disintegrated by 1980.


### The Ahmadiyya Movement

The Ahmadiyya Movement started in India in 1889. Its founder, Mirza Ghulam Ahmad, saw himself as the *Madhi* (the messianic savior of Islam). His aim was to bring reformation and revival to Islam. Ahmad's beliefs were expressed in his book *Barahim-I-Ahmadtah*.

Dr. Mufti Muhammad Sadiq brought the Ahmadiyya movement to the United States in 1921. Sadiq's original intention was to convert Islamic immigrants to the movement, but he experienced great success among African Americans.

The first American convert was Alexander Russell Webb. He was instrumental in the spread of the faith in the United States. In terms of evangelism, the Ahmadiyyas are among the most aggressive Islamic denomination. Because of Mirza Ghulam Ahmad's claim to be the Madhi, orthodox sects do not regard the Ahmadiyyas as truly Islamic.


### The Nubian Islamic Hebrews

In 1967, Isa Muhammad organized a group he called the Ansar Pure Sufi. Later, he referred to the group as Nubians. In 1969, he renamed the group the Nubian Islamic Hebrews. Muhammad officially founded the Ansar sect in 1970. In 1975, he changed the name of the sect to the Ansaru Allah Community.

Isa Muhammad incorporated many of the teachings of Elijah Muhammad and Noble Drew Ali into his theology. His followers believed him to be the great-grandson of a Sudanese man named Muhammad Ahmed ibn Abd'ullah—believed by Isa Muhammad to be the *Khaliyfa* (the expected successor to the prophet Muhammad). Muhammad claims to have been born in Omduram, Sudan, in 1945, yet he has an American birth certificate that names him Dwight York.

Isa Muhammad's background includes several name changes. As a teenager he changed his name to Isa abd'ALLAH ibn Abu Bakr Muhammad. In the mid-'60s he changed his name to Imam Isa Al Mahdi. In 1969, he changed his name to Assayid Al-Imam Isa Al-Hadi Al-Mahdi. In 1990, he changed his name to As Sayyid Isa al Haada al-Mahda.

In 1973, Isa Muhammad visited Mecca, Egypt and the Sudan. While there, he paid homage to the tomb of Al-Mahdi in Omduram (the African who defeated the armies of the British Empire). He also visited Al-Mahdi's family and Aba Island (the stronghold of the Ansar sect). Muhammad took pictures of himself in all the places he visited, to back up his claim to be of Sudanese origin. He later claimed that Al-Mahdi had come to America, married an African-American woman (Isa's mother) and returned to Sudan after Isa was born.

When Al-Mahdi's family got wind of Isa Muhammad's claims, they were furious. At first they intended to file suit against Isa Muhammad, but later, Al-Sadiq Al-Mahdi, the political leader of the family, decided against the suit. He saw an advantage in having an American following. Al-Sadiq Al-Mahdi later visited the Brooklyn headquarters and conferred legitimacy on the sect.

The Nubian Islamic Hebrews believe that the origin of the Nubian (Black) race goes back to Adam and Eve (Hawwah). They have developed their own twist on the "curse on Ham" myth. For them, Ham tried to commit sodomy with his drunk and naked father, Noah. The result was Noah's curse upon Canaan that turned his skin pale. Thus the Canaanites became the father of all pale-skinned races. Some Nubians intermarried with the outcast children of Canaan and produced:

- ❖ The Chinese
- ❖ The East Indians
- ❖ The Eskimos
- ❖ The Indonesians
- ❖ The Japanese
- ❖ The Koreans
- ❖ The Malayans
- ❖ The Pakistanis
- ❖ The Sicilians

Though these races are considered mixed, they are regarded as Black.

The Nubian Islamic Hebrews also believe that two additional nations came from Ibraahiym (Abraham). They were the descendants of Ishmael (the Ishmaelites) and the descendants of Isaac (the Israelites). Like the Israelites who were in Egyptian bondage, the Ishmaelites were held in American bondage for four hundred years. Out of this experience came the Nubians (Black people) of North America and the Caribbean. Because of their parallel experience with the Israelites, the American Nubians consider themselves to be Hebrews.

They believe that the beginning of their sect in 1970 was the opening of the seventh seal in Revelation 8:1.

Basically, the theology of the Nubian Islamic Hebrews is a mix of Christian, Islamic and Jewish beliefs.

MAINLINE: Most mainline American Muslims (90 percent) are Sunnis. However, many of them still have sympathies for the Black Nationalist orientation.

# FURTHER READING

Bailey, Randall C. and Jacquelyn Grant. *The Recovery of Black Presence: An Interdisciplinary Exploration—Essays in Honor of Dr. Charles B. Copher.* Nashville: Abingdon, 1995.

———. *For My People: Black Theology and the Black Church.* Maryknoll, New York: Orbis, 1984.

———. *God of the Oppressed.* New York: Seabury, 1975.

Copher, Charles B. "Three Thousand Years of Biblical Interpretation with Reference to Black Peoples." In *African American Religious Studies.* Ed. by Gayraud S. Wilmore. Durham and London: Duke University Press, 1989.

Davis, Don L. *Black and Human: Rediscovering King as a Resource for Black Theology and Ethics.* (Forthcoming.)

Ellis, Carl F. Jr. "Afrocentrism and Christianity: Complement or Conflict?" In *Urban Family,* Summer 1995, pp. 15-16.

Johnson, John L. *The Black Biblical Heritage.* Nashville: Winston-Derek, 1993.

Lincoln, C. Eric and Lawrence H. Mamiya. *The Black Church in the African American Experience.* Durham, NC: Duke University Press, 1990.

McCray, Walter Arthur. *The Black Presence in the Bible and the Table of Nations Genesis 10.1-32.* Chicago: Black Light Fellowship, 1990.

———. *The Black Presence in the Bible: Discovering the Black and African Identity of Biblical Persons and Nations (Teachers Guide).* Chicago: Black Light Fellowship, 1990.

———. *A Rationale for Black Christian Literature.* Chicago: National Black Students Conference, 1985.

McKissic, William Dwight. *Beyond Roots: In Search of Blacks in the Bible.* Wenonah, NJ: Renaissance Productions, 1990.

Mosely, William. *What Color Was Jesus?* Chicago: African American Images, 1987.

Pew Research Center. *Muslims Americans.* See http://pewresearch.org/assets/pdf/muslim-americans.pdf. Washington, D.C., 2007.

Usry, Glen and Craig S. Keener. *Black Man's Religion: Can Christianity Be Afro-centric?* Downers Grove, IL: InterVarsity Press, 1996.

WE OUGHT TO seek in every way we can to find methods of evangelism that are sensitive to and informed by Muslim thought and experience. We ought to research and find the best and most basic tools available to reach out to Muslims with the Gospel.

Tools such as Roland Mullers's *Tools for Muslim Evangelism*, Fouad Elias Accad's *Building Bridges* and Lyle Vander Werff's *Christian Mission to Muslims* (Rereleased in 2000) are a good place to start. Resources such as Dudley Woodberry's *Muslims & Christians on the Emmaus Road*, William Saal's *Reaching Muslims for Christ*, and Gordon D. Nickel's *Peaceable Witness Among Muslims* may also provide you with some practical ways to think of Christian-Muslim relationships and witnessing to Muslims.

An especially helpful tool for use with evangelizing those showing affinity to the Black Muslims is Dr. Smith's booklet *Louis Farrakhan and the Nation of Islam: Background and Beliefs*. This booklet details some of the central concepts and tenets of the Nation, and provides clear biblical answers to their ideology and theology. (Copies of this booklet are available through Dr. Smith at pastorrcsmith@juno.com.)

Discovering pertinent and relevant materials for evangelism among Muslims is always a welcome and important task. The William Carey Library, associated with the U.S. Center for World Mission, would be a good starting place to find resources, videos or tapes regarding the challenge and practice of evangelizing and planting churches among Muslims.

# INDEX

# Scripture Index